The Inspirational Teacher

Become a teacher who truly inspires students to learn and grow! This best-selling book—from Routledge and FranklinCovey, the company that brought you *The 7 Habits of Highly Effective People*—is filled with practical and heartfelt advice that will resonate with teachers at all stages of their careers. The book will guide you through a simple four-step process to building high-trust relationships and unleashing the greatness within all students.

This timely new edition includes updated references and inspirational quotes throughout, as well as chapter reflection questions to help you make the most of what you read. In addition, several of the questionnaires and reflection tools from the book are also available on our website (www.routledge.com/9781138906242) as free eResources, so that you can easily print and use them in your own classroom.

Gary McGuey, a former educator and athletic director, has spent the past decade traveling across the globe to visit schools and work with administrators, educators, and students. Gary is a former director of the Teens Division for FranklinCovey and created the first curriculum related to *The 7 Habits of Highly Effective Teens*. He is a sought-after keynote speaker on topics related to leadership, team building, and student empowerment.

Lonnie Moore is a former award-winning middle school and high school math teacher. Lonnie now works with FranklinCovey as a training consultant. He has facilitated more than 1,400 workshops, keynotes, and seminars. As a part of the FranklinCovey Education Practice, he contributed to the creation of The Leader in Me school improvement process. This powerful process is being implemented in more than 2,000 schools globally.

The Inspirational Teacher

Second Edition

Gary McGuey and Lonnie Moore

Routledge
Taylor & Francis Group
NEW YORK AND LONDON

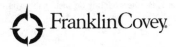

FranklinCovey

Second edition published 2016
by Routledge
711 Third Avenue, New York, NY 10017

and by Routledge
2 Park Square, Milton Park, Abingdon, Oxon, OX14 4RN

*Routledge is an imprint of the Taylor & Francis Group,
an informa business*

First edition published by Routledge, 2007

Library of Congress Cataloging-in-Publication Data
McGuey, Gary.
  The inspirational teacher/by Gary McGuey and Lonnie Moore.
    pages cm
  1. Teachers—Attitudes. 2. Teacher morale 3. Teacher-
student relationships. I. Moore, Lonnie. II. Title.
  LB2840.M385 2016
  371.102'3—dc23
  2015012718

ISBN: 978-1-138-90623-5 (hbk)
ISBN: 978-1-138-90624-2 (pbk)
ISBN: 978-1-315-69561-7 (ebk)

Typeset in Palatino
by Apex CoVantage, LLC

Printed and bound in the United States of America by
Edwards Brothers Malloy on sustainably sourced paper

Contents

eResources

Several of the tools and templates from the book are also available on our website so that you can print and use them in your own classroom. The material includes the following:

- ◆ Mission Statement Questionnaires
- ◆ Impact Trivia Sheets
- ◆ End-of-Chapter Reflection Questions

To download those items, go to the book product page, www.routledge.com/9781138906242. Then click on the tab that says "eResources" and select the files. They will begin downloading to your computer.

Foreword

The Inspirational Teacher aims to make any teacher, at any time, motivational and meaningful. I wish I had had a copy of it in my bag of tricks when I began my educational journey. Instead I had thick textbooks on pedagogy written by stodgy professors. Without Gary and Lonnie's practical blueprint, I felt like I was flying without a net and learning lessons from my mistakes. And although I have been hailed as an inspiring teacher, if truth be told, I am a much better student. My most inspirational teachers, ironically, started out as the most unmotivated students. Luckily, my students—the Freedom Writers—have not only inspired me but also are an inspiration to struggling students and talented teachers alike. But their inspiration was neither innate nor immediate.

When I was a kid, I loved school—so much so that when I was covered from head to toe with poison oak and my eyes were sealed shut, my mother made me stay home from school. To a fanatical fifth grader, missing school was a fate worse than death. Even though I was so swollen I couldn't see, and was under doctor's orders, missing one day of school meant that I wouldn't have perfect attendance. Nor would I receive that coveted ribbon.

Yes, I was *that* kid. The one who got to school extra early to help my teacher set up. I stayed after school to erase the chalkboards, too. My pencils were sharpened, I reveled in trips to the library, and my homework was turned in early. I even did extra-credit work. And I didn't just raise my hand; I raised both. My parents helped me with class projects, they volunteered for the PTA, and our refrigerator was covered with my handiwork. My assignments were adorned with gold stars, words of encouragement from my teachers like "Dynamite," and even the worm in the apple sticker was smiling.

Oh, how I loved school. My students, however, did not. I was in for a rude awakening when I bounced into Room 203 at Wilson High School like a perky cheerleader and my disgruntled students came in after the tardy bell rang. Unlike me, they did not need a doctor's note to miss class. They didn't have writing utensils. Or books. And wouldn't be caught dead in the library. They'd rather use Cliff Notes than read a book cover to cover. And, worse yet, they raised a finger, rather than their hand, and it wasn't to answer a question. When I called home to talk to a parent, I rarely got a reply. Many of their parents worked two or three jobs and didn't participate in the school bake sale because they were too busy putting food on their own table.

Immediately, I realized that I had learned how to teach only kids like me in the halls of academia, not the tough teenagers sitting before me. Rather than dive into the literary lessons from the canon that I had meticulously prepared, I realized that my students hated reading and hated writing. I wondered how I could motivate them to pick up a book and find themselves within the pages. How could I engage them to leave a legacy with their words?

In an act of desperation, I sought help from my administrators. Unfortunately, that didn't help, either. My principal told me that I had all the apathetic students—disciplinary transfers, the soon-to-drop-out, and remedial readers who scored well below the standard scores for the school. It was clear that he expected me to be a glorified babysitter and to simply teach to the test.

Refusing to teach to the test, I decided to teach to them. I believed that my students were more than the sum of their scores. Somehow, someway, I would try to inspire them.

My "aha" moment as a teacher came when I asked my students to find the courage to change. I wanted to wipe the slate clean. I wanted my students to start over. I wanted school to be their refuge. It didn't matter that some had a 0.5 GPA or that others had been kicked out of every school they ever attended. Starting right then, starting right there, I wanted to inspire them to change. And to do so, we raised that plastic champagne glass, filled with sparkling apple cider, and made a Toast for Change.

And change they did.

In the process, I was inspired to change, too. I would become a better teacher. I would not teach to a test. I would not treat my students as if they were one-size-fits-all. I would be sensitive to the fact that not everyone had a childhood like mine. I would not judge my students on the basis of what their parents did or didn't do. To be an inspirational teacher, I would need to make learning come to life. I would have to make reading relevant. I would teach that writing would right wrongs. I would inspire my students to come in early and leave late, to raise their hands, to think critically, to question authority, and to love Room 203. As a result, my students went on to become voracious readers and acclaimed authors. Once I recognized the importance of seeing my students for who they were and where they came from, Room 203 became a home, and my storytellers became a family. Yes, they are now *those* students.

Twenty years later, when I reflect upon my first day as a teacher, I smile at my naiveté. I remember how I enthusiastically studied the principles of pedagogy in college and believed that I was ready to change the world on day one. Yet, when I stepped into Room 203, I quickly discovered how woefully unprepared I was for the challenges of working with vulnerable youth. Once I figured out how to inspire them, they in turn inspired others. In fact, many of them have become inspirational educators themselves. Daisy, who entered my class with the label of "runaway," is now working with troubled teens in middle school. Ramon used to dodge bullets and bury friends, but he is now a teacher in an even tougher neighborhood than the one he grew up in. Oscar's father never volunteered for the PTA or visited my class on Back-to-School night. His father had a third-grade education and came to this country undocumented, but he believed in the concept of the American Dream for his son. Now his son, Oscar, is a principal of a school where the majority of his students look like him and come from where he comes from. He inspires them to dream. And dream big.

Inspiring teachers change students' lives. Inspiring students change ours. While my classroom has changed over the years, I am still honored to call myself a teacher. As a lifelong learner, I too, need professional development, and that is how I had the privilege of experiencing Gary and Lonnie's passion and purpose. I may be a teacher to many, but to them I am their student. Yes, I was *that* student. I raised my hand. I asked questions. I stayed late to learn from Lonnie. And Gary gave me the proverbial gold star. I was inspired.

The strategies and tools within *The Inspirational Teacher* enable you to reach your potential as an educator and to stay true to your calling. The book will enable you to build a classroom where students feel safe, secure and can take risks, where they will feel like a family.

Gary and Lonnie's wisdom about the art of inspiration continues to inspire through their writings. Their dedication and expertise in teaching are evident on each and every page. My hope is that each new teacher will read this book, garner tips of the trade, and feel more prepared as they enter their first classroom. And for experienced teachers, may this book rejuvenate you and remind you why you chose this noble profession.

—Erin Gruwell
Teacher/Founder of the Freedom Writers

Meet the Authors

Gary McGuey, a former educator and athletic director, has spent the past decade traveling to all 50 states, as well as internationally. He has visited thousands of schools and has worked with administrators, educators, and students.

Gary is the former director of the Teens Division of Franklin-Covey and created the first curriculum related to *The 7 Habits of Highly Effective Teens*. Gary has also been an Executive Coach at the White House.

Gary authored *The Mentor: Leadership Trumps Bullying*, which provides a proactive approach to reducing bullying issues in schools. He is the coauthor of *The Inspirational Teacher*, which deals with the power of building relationships with your students.

Gary is a highly respected speaker who brings the rare mix of knowledge, humor, and wisdom to every engagement. *"Learn it, Live it, Give it!"* is the message Gary conveys to his audiences. Through a variety of hands-on interactive sessions, participants are encouraged and challenged to continue the process of leadership development. He is a sought-after keynote speaker on topics related to leadership, team building, and student empowerment.

Gary lives in the Finger Lakes region of New York with his wife, Christina, and their children.

Lonnie Moore is a former middle school and high school math teacher. In just his third year in the classroom, he was recognized as Mainstream Teacher of the Year in Pinellas County, Florida.

In 2000, after nine years in the classroom, Lonnie joined Franklin-Covey as a training consultant. Since then he has facilitated more than 1,400 workshops, keynotes, and seminars. As a part of the FranklinCovey Education Practice, he contributed to the creation of The Leader in Me school improvement process. This powerful process is being implemented in more than 2,000 schools globally.

Lonnie has worked with schools from New York City to Honolulu to London, England. Lonnie's experience working with groups of diverse backgrounds has given him a unique and clear vision of what it takes to create impactful programs within schools.

His dynamic and entertaining style makes his presentations fun, challenging, and thought provoking. In addition to *The Inspirational Teacher*, he is the author of *The High-Trust Classroom: Raising Achievement from the Inside-Out*. His training topics include The Leader in Me, student motivation, life management, stress management, becoming an inspirational teacher, creating high-trust classrooms, and success training for teens.

Lonnie's hobbies include running, biking, and swimming, and he has completed more than 100 triathlons, including the Ironman. He has been married to Margie since 1988 and has two daughters, Jessica and Lauren. Lonnie and his family reside in Tampa, Florida.

Acknowledgments

This book would have not been possible without the loving support and encouragement of our families: Gary's wife, Christina, and their children, Sean, Devin, Liam, Alyssa, Caitlin, and Tot, and Lonnie's wife, Margie, and their children, Jessica and Lauren.

We would also like to recognize our own "Inspirational Teachers," those who inspired us to become educators, Barbara Thornton in Pinellas County, Florida, and Ed Duffield in North York, Ontario. These two legendary educators believed in and valued every one of their students and challenged students to reach their potential every day.

Although many great leaders and teachers have contributed to the shaping of *The Inspirational Teacher*, we would like to especially thank Sean Covey, Muriel Summers, Stephen M. R. Covey, Erin Gruwell, Dr. Stephen Uebbing, Tony Contos, Susan Leger-Ferraro, Jon Gordon, Michael Fullan, Shelly Catrino, Jeff Tolson, Linda Crain, Chuck Farnsworth, and Annie Oswald. We would also like to thank the thousands of students and educators we have been privileged to work with over the past two decades.

Last, our deepest gratitude goes to our true inspirational teachers—our parents, Dennis and Edith McGuey and Lonnie Sr. and Jane Moore.

Part I

The Foundation of the Inspirational Teacher

The mediocre teacher tells. The good teacher explains. The superior teacher demonstrates. The great teacher inspires.

—William Arthur Ward

1

Introduction

In everyone's life, at some time, our inner
fire goes out.
It is then burst into flame by the encounter
with another human being.
We should all be thankful for those people
who rekindle our inner spirit.

—Albert Schweitzer

Today's young people are constantly faced with challenging life choices, choices associated with peer pressure, school, bullying, drugs, family, and relationships. Though the pain and frustration are real, solutions to these challenges are not so clear. The one potential constant that could offer them hope is an inspirational teacher. Without question, a major contributing factor to staying on the right path is having an individual who inspires us to make the right choices. Many times a great teacher is the catalyst or source of this inspiration.

What makes a great teacher?

Think back to all the teachers you had in school. How many of them would you define as "inspirational"? Our experiences show that most people can think of only two. That's two teachers in your entire educational experience. Despite the fact that

FIGURE 1.1 The Inspirational Teacher Process

this number is surprisingly low, the formula for success is proven. This formula includes how teachers:

- ◆ Model Principles
- ◆ Demonstrate Respect
- ◆ Genuinely Listen
- ◆ Build High-Trust Relationships

Model Principles + Demonstrate Respect + Genuinely Listen = High-Trust Relationships

Given this formula, are you an inspirational teacher?

Today's Reality

The reality within education is that nearly half of all new teachers leave the profession within the first five years. Why does this happen? New teachers enter the profession with all their excitement and desire to become the best teacher possible. They have chosen this profession to make a difference in the lives of young people. As new teachers, they have studied many educational philosophies and researched the top educational-thought leaders. They have observed the classrooms of veteran teachers and attended various professional development "in services" required of new staff. On the first day of school, they are prepared and ready to go. Some may even feel they are on their way to become the next "Teacher of the Year."

Suddenly, the reality of teaching hits them. The school year begins, and the real challenges unfold. From our experiences, we have categorized these challenges into three areas (see checklist).

Challenges of Being a New Teacher

Classroom Discipline:

♦ Do you have established classroom guidelines (we do not use the word "rules" in this book)?
♦ How do you deal with challenging students?
♦ Have you established agreed-upon consequences for students who do not follow the guidelines?
♦ How will you communicate with the parents?

Classroom Management:

♦ Have you developed procedures to help make your class more efficient?
♦ Are you well prepared?
♦ Are you on time?
♦ Are you sensitive to the various learning styles of your students?
♦ Do you give your students a voice to help establish the culture of the classroom?

Support:

- ◆ Do you have an (effective) mentor teacher?
- ◆ Do you have the opportunity to spend time with and learn from your colleagues?
- ◆ Does the district offer a teacher induction program?
- ◆ Does the principal have frequent meetings with you?

The Many Roles of Teaching

To become an inspirational teacher requires a holistic mindset. A teacher in the twenty-first century must be equipped with the proper attitude and skills to handle today's realities. No longer is a teacher just a teacher. Today a teacher must wear many hats. A teacher must be a counselor, parent, advocate, mediator, confidant, adviser, and more. Every beginning teacher has the potential to take on these new roles. Each of these roles requires new and better skills. Unfortunately, during the hiring process, many administrators assume new teachers have already developed these skills. During the teacher induction process, these skills often do not receive the attention they truly deserve. Given this, the high teacher-turnover numbers are not surprising.

Most educators agree that the most important factor in determining students' success in the classroom is the degree to which teachers value them. In Dr. John Hattie's book *Visible Learning for Teachers* (2012), he shares his findings, which are based on more than 800 meta-analyses of 50,000 research articles, 150,000 effect sizes, and 240 million students. The result of this massive study has become a handbook for many school leaders. In fact, one reviewer said that Hattie has identified the holy grail of teaching and it is the quality of interaction between the teacher and student. By applying the strategies and tools within this book, you too, will build high-trust relationships.

The most important factor in determining students' success in the classroom is the degree to which teachers value them.

Effective Teachers

How do we define an "effective" teacher? People who are effective in any capacity are those who continually achieve their goals and continually strive to improve themselves and everyone around them. Teachers' goals are to lead students to understand course content, apply concepts to life experiences, and empower their students to make good choices and become lifelong learners. Teachers who develop trusting relationships (a caring classroom culture) combined with deep knowledge of their subject (academics) will leave an everlasting impact on all of their students. This is truly the art of teaching.

> **Teachers who develop trusting relationships (a caring classroom culture) combined with deep knowledge of their subject (academics) will leave an everlasting impact on all of their students.**

Effective teachers are:

◆ Caring
◆ Continuous Learners
◆ Dedicated
◆ Engaging
◆ Organized
◆ Forgiving
◆ Resourceful
◆ Empowering

Why Teach?

> The two most important days in your life are the day you are born and the day you find out why.
>
> —Mark Twain

Why did you choose to become a teacher?

Most teachers would say they have a passion to change lives and make a difference. They have a vision of what it takes to succeed in our society and want to share this vision with the next generation. Although their intentions are noble, sincere, and potentially heroic, without a solid personal foundation and skill set teachers are destined for mediocrity.

We have found that most educators fall into one of two categories. Many teachers see themselves as professionals, while others see teaching as only their job.

Do You Have a Job, or Are You a Professional Educator?

Sadly, there are teachers who have the job mindset. While they fight through the drudgery of Monday mornings, they celebrate upcoming weekends. They say things like, "Oh my, it's Monday again" or "TGIF!" Many of them actually have a countdown calendar tracking the days until the next holiday or summer break. Imagine the message this sends to students: "My teachers are counting down the days until they don't have to be with me anymore."

Teachers with the job mindset typically do the minimum and rarely participate on committees or in afterschool events. They often cite student misbehavior, unsupportive parents, and out-of-touch administrators as the cause of their classroom challenges. Most likely, there was a time when these teachers had a vision of becoming professional educators. Their intent was genuine, but their resolve was not. Something happened to their mindset. For some reason they've lost that sparkle in their eye. Perhaps the sparkle has faded over a couple of years, or maybe it's taken 25 years. Regardless, they have lost their passion, and their students feel it everyday. Students feel their reactivity or lackadaisical attitude toward daily preparation and relationship building.

On the other hand, there are the professional educators. They have found their calling. Being centered on their mission, they are perfectly aligned to inspire everyday. They seem to have an unending curiosity, which drives them to enthusiastically attend conferences, read journals, and seek new ways to unleash the greatness within every student. They lead committees and help organize many afterschool events. Their passion is overflowing, and parents strive to get their children in these teachers' classes.

Are you a professional educator, or do you have a job?

These three questions will help you with this personal assessment.

1. What is your daily impact on students and your school culture?
2. What would your students, parents, and colleagues feel if you resigned today?
3. Do your behaviors match your mission?

In this book, you will have an opportunity to reconnect with your purpose as a professional educator. You will assess your current level of classroom effectiveness and professional happiness. You will also learn what it takes to become an inspirational teacher and deeply connect with even the most challenging students.

Reducing Teacher Turnover

School district administrators understand the time and money required to recruit and train new teachers. Given the alarming rates of teacher turnover in many districts, it's fortunate that robust teacher induction programs are proving to be an effective means of decreasing the number of teachers who leave the district. Although there are many aspects of new teacher training, modeling, respecting, and listening are rarely given the attention they truly deserve. The inspirational teacher process will meet the often overlooked skill of creating high-trust learning environments.

Sustaining the process within this book will help you become an inspirational teacher; you will stay true to your mission and your students will sense your passion every day. However, you must be patient and follow the four levels of *Modeling Principles, Demonstrating Respect, Genuine Listening,* and *Building High-Trust Relationships.* Continue to reflect, and continue to grow. This is an educational journey that never ends. Through this process you will become an inspirational teacher.

Those who choose not to internalize and apply the principles aligned with this process will inevitably begin the downward spiral of becoming more stressed out and increasingly cynical. Unfortunately, over time, these same teachers will gradually become disconnected from their mission and become the "negative teachers" who inhabit schools. The good news is that anyone (even teachers who feel this has become a "job") who applies the principles aligned with becoming an inspirational teacher will reconnect with her purpose and will ultimately leave a positive impact on her students.

Expected Outcomes for the Inspirational Teacher

When the inspirational teacher process is followed with fidelity, teachers will:

- ◆ Establish a culture of empowerment
- ◆ Have more influence with students and colleagues
- ◆ Inspire many students whom others may have given up on
- ◆ Experience enhanced relationships with students, colleagues, and parents
- ◆ Have improved communication
- ◆ Have a continued connection to their passion as educators
- ◆ Feel more balanced both professionally and personally
- ◆ Make education a lifelong career.

Raheen's Discovery Sixth-Grade Inspirational Teacher

Raheen was a very troubled sixth grader with poor attendance and poor grades. In fact, for most of his time in school he was placed in a "behavioral development class." In an effort to get Raheen back into a mainstream class, the school placed him in the class of Mrs. Bryant, a no-nonsense teacher who was there to "teach" curriculum, with little regard to building relationships with her students.

Mrs. Bryant knew of Raheen's reputation and was not happy to have him as a student. The results were predictably negative. After less than a month, Raheen was placed back in the behavioral development class. The documentation stated that he was "not prepared" for integration into mainstream classes.

The next semester, after a few parent/principal discussions, Mrs. O'Neal, a well-respected and admired teacher (by both staff and students) was asked if she would let Raheen be part of her class. Raheen was initially confrontational and extremely challenging. He would come in late and disrupt the class. Mrs. O'Neal stayed true to her principles; her response and demeanor were pleasant and inviting, yet firm and fair. If Raheen was going to improve his attitude, then Mrs. O'Neal's patience and modeling were going to be the key. She made an effort to learn more about Raheen and gave him the extra attention he needed. Raheen began to realize that his teacher cared about him and wanted to help him succeed, not only in the classroom but outside school as well.

Over the next semester, Raheen began to see and treat his teacher differently. He realized that she truly valued and respected him as a person. He started to act according to the same principles shown to him by Mrs. O'Neal. His attitude and behavior toward school improved. Mrs. O'Neal's modeling and relationship-building skills were paying off. Raheen became a successful mainstream student.

Chapter 1 Summary

Great teachers inspire their students daily. They follow the formula of the inspirational teacher: *Modeling Principles, Demonstrating Respect, Genuinely Listening*, and establishing *High-Trust Relationships*. Research shows that once the social-emotional aspect of a classroom is established, academics will follow.

The most important factor in determining students' success is the degree to which teachers value them. Dr. John Hattie's book, *Visible Learning for Teachers,* echoes our findings. The key to teaching is the interaction between the student and the teacher.

Inspirational teachers view teaching as a profession, not a job. They stay connected to their mission and ensure that their behaviors match their mission.

By following the inspirational teacher process, teachers can establish a culture of empowerment in which students feel valued and respected. They will inspire and challenge their students to reach and exceed their own expectations.

Inspirational teachers will make education a lifelong career and, over time, will make an incredible difference in thousands of students' lives.

Chapter 1 Reflection Questions

1. In what ways do you model principles daily?

2. Do you have high-trust relationships with colleagues and students?

3. For you, is teaching a job or a profession? Why?

The Personal Mission Statement

We detect rather than invent our missions.

—Victor Frankl, *Man's Search for Meaning*

The foundation of all inspirational teachers is a well-designed personal mission statement. Clearly defining one's vision and purpose makes all the difference. A mission statement is a self-proclaimed constitution for how you will lead your life, both personal and professional. This will become your most impactful decision-making tool; inspirational teachers connect to their mission daily and center themselves on what truly matters.

> **Inspirational teachers connect to their mission daily and center themselves on what truly matters.**

A great mission statement uniquely expresses who you are, what you want to become, how you want to be remembered. It becomes the basis for making decisions. At the conclusion of the mission statement process you will have an initial draft of your personal mission statement; you will have a greater sense of clarity and a renewed commitment to your profession. As Victor Frankl so eloquently noted, "We detect rather invent" our mission statements.

It may take several re-writes to come up with a statement that truly inspires you.

Mission Statement Guidelines

A great mission statement should:

1. Inspire you.
2. Present who you are and what principles you value.
3. Clarify what is important to you.

Default versus Design

> To be a teacher. And to be known for inspiring my students to be more than they thought they could be.
> —Oprah Winfrey's personal mission statement

While some people are planners, others are not. While some people rigidly adhere to their daily checklist, others are comfortable trying to remember important events and just rolling with whatever happens throughout the day. Some people are fine going with the flow, often allowing life to happen to them or living by default. Countless experts on human effectiveness say that living each day with intention will produce exponentially greater results. The simple habit of intentionally designing each day, week, and year of your life can have a huge impact on your happiness, balance, and overall sense of accomplishment.

Do You Live by Default or by Design?

Did You Become a Teacher by Default or Design?

Like most educators, you may say, "Yes, I do live by design." However, once you begin to reflect more deeply, you may realize that you often live day to day, hour to hour, or even crisis to crisis. Intentionally designing your day or week is great, but what if you designed your life? How far into your future can you see—a month, a year, five years, or longer? Your personal mission statement serves as a compass for your life; it is your foundation. This foundation provides clarity and allows you to focus on what truly matters most in your life.

> Your personal mission statement serves as a compass for your life; it is your foundation. This foundation provides clarity and allows you to focus on what truly matters most in your life.

The Qualities of a Personal Mission Statement

◆ It inspires you.
◆ It states what principles you value.
◆ It clarifies your purpose.

Your mission statement should capture what is important to you. Your values, your priorities, and your vision of your future are just under the surface of your written mission statement. Many people may choose to express everything in writing, while others may create a mission statement as a symbol or motto for their life. See the sample statements on pages 18–19.

Destiny is a not a matter of chance; it is a matter of choice.

Sample Personal Mission Statements

I will live a life true to my values and beliefs. I will not allow the outside influences of others to pull me down. I will constantly strive to learn and enrich my body, mind, and spirit.

At the end of my life I will look back with a clear conscience. I will have no regrets and no "what if's."

I shall conquer untruth by truth. And in resisting untruth, I shall put up with all suffering. -Mahatma Ghandi

FIGURE 2.1 Sample Personal Mission Statements

In my everyday life
I will strive to make
a difference with both
my family and my students.

I will leave everything
a little better than
I found it.

To inspire everyone,
everyday.

To make my
family proud.

FIGURE 2.1 (Continued)

Benefits of a Personal Mission Statement

> When you know what you want and you want it bad enough, you'll find a way to get it.
>
> —Jim Rohn

A personal mission statement:

- ◆ Provides clarity.
- ◆ Centers you on your purpose as an educator.
- ◆ Fosters healthy relationships.
- ◆ Guides your day-to-day decisions.
- ◆ Gives you permission to say "no" to things not aligned with your personal mission statement.

How to Develop a Personal Mission Statement

> The greatest thing in this world is not so much where we are, but in what direction we are moving.
>
> —O. W. Holmes

The development of a personal mission statement is not a simple process and should not be completed quickly. Time, effort, and reflection are required in this process.

Most people are too busy living to take the time to consider their direction in life. When asked, "What are you willing to die for?" the most common answer is "Family." However, these same people admit that they do not live every day as if family were the most important thing in their life. In fact, those who matter most to us tend to receive the brunt of our frustration. This is perhaps the greatest irony of life. Those that we love the most often receive the least.

As you begin the mission statement process, find a quiet place to write. Allow yourself plenty of time, and don't rush. The depth and quality of your mission statement will be proportionate to the time and effort invested.

In High-Trust Schools . . .

Teachers constantly spoke about the importance of *respecting* parents, regardless of their background or education achievement. Although many students came from troubled homes, teachers did not attempt to distance themselves from their students or families. (Bryk and Schneider, *Trust in Schools* [New York: Russell Sage Foundation, 2002], p. 84)

Teachers' active encouragement of parents, coupled with their demonstrated personal regard for the children, opened up possibilities for teachers and parents to negotiate complementary roles in the children's education. (Bryk and Schneider, *Trust in Schools* [New York: Russell Sage Foundation, 2002], p. 86)

As Bryk and Schneider (2002) emphasize, under condition of power asymmetry with poor parents, vulnerable and unconfident in their relationship to schools, it is incumbent on principals and teachers to reach out, be empathetic, and create possibilities for parent involvement. When they do, as Bryk and Schneider found, greater connection is made with parents and students, and achievement goes up.

Michael Fullan, *Leadership and Sustainability, System Thinkers in Action* (Newbury Park, CA: Corwin Press, 2005), pp. 60–61.

Mission Statement Questionnaire

The following questions will assist you in detecting and drawing out your talents, goals, beliefs, and values. The final assignment in this process will be the creation of your personal mission statement.

Question 1: Identify talents.

Create a list of your skills or gifts. (Examples: artist, public speaking, writing, humor, leading others, analytical thinking, athletic, technological)

Talent 1: _____

Talent 2: _____

Talent 3: _____

Talent 4: _____

Talent 5: _____

Question 2: Identify areas of passion or desire to impact.

Create a list of things you are passionate about and where you would like to make an impact. (Examples: education of young children, community service, school leadership, personal fitness, relationships, and personal growth, reading, poetry)

Question 3: Clarify values/set boundaries.

Create a list of your values. This should serve as a set of guidelines or personal promises by which you will lead your life. Values could include words such as honesty, trust, hard work, love, integrity, fun, togetherness, helpful.

Question 4: If money were not an issue, what would you choose to do?

Question 5: Who has had the most impact on your growth and development?

Question 6: List the most important people in your life.

Question 7: At your retirement dinner, what would you want people to say about you and your teaching career?

Question 8: What is your ultimate goal in life?

Question 9: What are the greatest obstacles to your becoming an inspirational teacher?

Question 10: How will you overcome those obstacles?

Personal Mission Statement

Rough Draft

The next step in detecting your mission in life is to write your first rough draft. In the space below, allow your thoughts to flow. Do not worry about grammar or sentence structure. Simply get your thoughts on paper. Prior to beginning, reflect back on your answers to the questions on the previous pages, and then answer the question "What is my mission?"

_____

_____

_____

_____

_____

_____

_____

_____

Congratulations!

Now that you've challenged yourself and answered the questions on the previous pages, we would like to say "Congratulations!" With this initial draft, you are establishing a foundation that will keep you on track for becoming an inspirational teacher. This powerful tool will define your purpose and help keep you focused on what matters most.

Your completed mission statement should be visible to you. Take a few minutes every morning and evening to center and reflect around your mission.

The question we need to ask ourselves every day is this:

Do my behaviors match my mission?

Chapter 2 Summary

Inspirational teachers live their life by design. After deep thought and research, they have intentionally chosen to teach. This choice is a derivative of their personal mission statement, which expresses who they are, what they want to become, and how they wish to be remembered. Their personal mission statement serves as a compass and gives them permission to say "yes" to some things and "no" to others.

A great mission statement has the following characteristics:

◆ It inspires you.
◆ It defines who you are and what principles you value.
◆ It clarifies what is most important to you.

Your personal mission statement should be placed in a visible location. We suggest that you take a few minutes each morning to center yourself on your mission and that you ask this question twice a day (once in the morning, and once at night): "Do my behaviors match my mission?"

eRESOURCES

Chapter 2 Reflection Questions

1. What is your personal mission statement?

2. Do your daily choices and behaviors align with your personal mission statement?
   Explain your answer.

3. Name three benefits of a personal mission statement.

   1.
   2.
   3.

The Classroom/Grade-Level Mission Statement

The most important action an effective teacher takes at the beginning of the year is creating a climate for learning.
—Mary Beth Blegan, former National Teacher of the Year

A classroom mission statement is created by both students and the teacher. By involving the students in this process, you will create a powerful set of classroom guidelines. These guidelines will represent the purpose, values, and intentions of both you and your students. It will tell everyone what you want, what you are about, and what you value as a class.

The power of the classroom mission statement has less to do with the end product and more to do with the process. By involving the students in this process, you help them feel a sense of ownership, commitment, and accountability.

The classroom mission statement should be created within the first three weeks of the school year and should be proudly displayed inside and outside the classroom. Remember, the first 3 weeks of school set up the next 33 weeks (3/33 formula).

The Four Steps to Creating a Classroom Mission Statement

Step 1: Hand out the Classroom Mission Statement Questionnaire, one per student. (See page 31–32.)

Step 2: Gather responses and share common themes with students.

Step 3: Start a whole-class discussion. At this point, you as the teacher facilitate a deeper discussion with regard to each of the common themes, thus creating a deeper sense of involvement and commitment in every student.

Step 4: Formulate the classroom mission statement. The classroom mission statement may take many forms. It can be expressed in writing, as a collage, or in any other form. This final product should be a class collaboration, and all students should feel that they have had input into its creation.

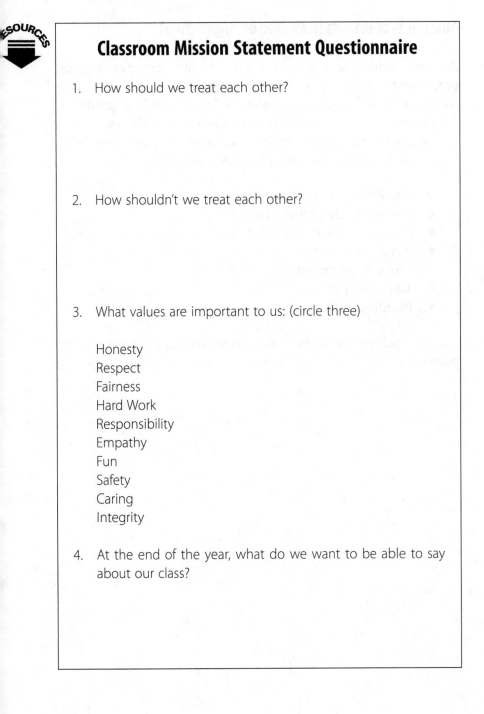

Classroom Mission Statement Questionnaire

1. How should we treat each other?

2. How shouldn't we treat each other?

3. What values are important to us: (circle three)

   Honesty
   Respect
   Fairness
   Hard Work
   Responsibility
   Empathy
   Fun
   Safety
   Caring
   Integrity

4. At the end of the year, what do we want to be able to say about our class?

Mission Statements in Middle or High School

At the middle school and high school level, we suggest grade-level or departmental mission statements. Use the same four questions, but change the word "classroom" to "grade" or "department." *Involving students in the process is the key.*

We also suggest that mission statements be created for other key areas and units around the school, including:

◆ The library or media center
◆ Parent-Teacher Organization
◆ Physical Education department
◆ Art department
◆ Music department
◆ The cafeteria
◆ Building maintenance

See the gallery of sample classroom mission statements on pages 31–32.

Examples of Classroom Mission Statements

We will respect others,
be kind, do our best, and believe
in ourselves to achieve
success in third grade.

Campbell's Campers are awesome
kids who love to learn and
want to become great leaders.

We lead by working together,
being responsible and fair every day.

We always do our best and work
together to fill everyone's bucket.

We are a class of leaders who
help others become leaders.

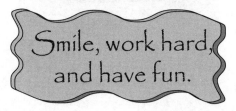

Smile, work hard,
and have fun.

FIGURE 3.1 Sample Classroom Mission Statements

We have a positive attitude
and strive for greatness every day.

We, Mr. Johnson's class, are here to learn and make
friends. We promise to be respectful, responsible,
and honest. We will be kind and stick up for others.
We will use the 7 habits and we won't
give up when things are hard.

P E
where we...
Learn to be fit.
Exercise daily.
Acitively participate.
Do what is right.

Room 205 Class Mission
Statement
Our mission is to be kind,
respectful, and responsible kids.
We will listen, learn,
teach each other, and have fun
in our classroom. We will do
our best to reach every goal
that we set for ourselves.

Mrs. Smith's Class Mission Statement
We promise to do our kindergarten best
to work together, play together, and
learn together each and every day!

FIGURE 3.1 (Continued)

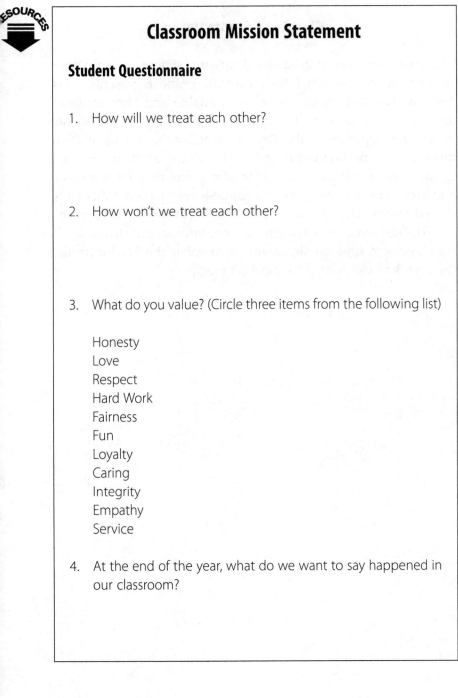

Classroom Mission Statement

Student Questionnaire

1. How will we treat each other?

2. How won't we treat each other?

3. What do you value? (Circle three items from the following list)

   Honesty
   Love
   Respect
   Hard Work
   Fairness
   Fun
   Loyalty
   Caring
   Integrity
   Empathy
   Service

4. At the end of the year, what do we want to say happened in our classroom?

Chapter 3 Summary

Classroom mission or grade-level mission statements empower students to choose what their class or grade represents. This mission statement holds people accountable and often replaces the need for class rules. The process of involving your students in the development is the key. A great leadership tip is "No involvement, no commitment." By involving students, we are establishing a culture where all students feel they have a voice and are valued. Classroom and grade-level mission statements should be proudly displayed inside and outside the classroom.

The first three weeks of school is the optimal time to establish the classroom mission statement. Remember the 3/33 formula; the first 3 weeks set up the next 33 weeks.

Chapter 3 Reflection Questions

1. How would you have students participate in the creation of a classroom or grade-level mission statement?

2. In your classroom or workspace, where is the best place to display the classroom or grade-level mission statement?

3. Which of the classroom mission statement examples do you find most meaningful?

Part II

Becoming an Inspirational Teacher

Every great dream begins with a dreamer. Always remember, you have within you the strength, the patience, and the passion to reach for the stars to change the world.

—Harriet Tubman

The Inspirational Teacher Process

The process of becoming an inspirational teacher follows the same timeless principles as the building of a pyramid. Pyramids are the most stable geometric forms because of their strong foundational bases. The enduring strength of a pyramid can be compared to the enduring strength, confidence, and skill of inspirational teachers.

The foundation of the inspirational teacher is a result of a connection to their values, passions, and talents. This foundation includes the development of both personal and classroom mission statements. While the educational mission statement focuses on "why" we chose this profession, the classroom mission statement is an empowering tool to provide guidelines and expectations for all students. Both of these mission statements provide

FIGURE II.1 The Inspirational Teacher Process

focus and direction and guide your day-to-day decisions. Once you have invested a few minutes every morning in reflecting, connecting, and centering yourself on your mission, you will have established the foundation for what is required to become an inspirational teacher.

The next three levels of the inspirational teacher process are modeling, respecting, and listening. The consistent application of the first three levels of the pyramid will ultimately result in trusting relationships.

Natural leaders know you cannot "make" anyone follow you; you must become a person whom people "want" to follow. The same is true in the classroom; by taking time to build your own foundation, by consistently modeling principles, by respecting both ourselves and our students, by demonstrating sincere listening skills, we achieve the desired goal of inspirational teaching.

4

Modeling Principles

Setting an example is not the main means of influencing another; it is the only means.

—Albert Einstein

Who has inspired you the most? Most likely it was a parent, teacher, family member, coach, or mentor. Why did these people inspire you? They inspired you because of who they are. They inspired by their actions and behaviors. They challenged, cared, supported, trusted, listened, and allowed you to take risks, (remember, failure is fertilizer). They not only believed in you but convinced you to believe in yourself. This is the ultimate goal of inspirational teaching.

But where does this skill of inspiring others come from? Are you born with it? Can this skill be learned? Without question, yes, the skills that allow us to build a culture where students feel valued can be developed and enhanced. Every person reading this book has the

Every person reading this book has the potential to become inspirational. However, the principles involved in becoming inspirational require hard work, patience, humility, and dedication. This is a lifelong process.

potential to become inspirational. However, the principles involved in becoming inspirational require hard work, patience, humility, and dedication. This is a lifelong process.

Most educators have received specialized training to prepare them for "how" to teach. They are taught pedagogy, lesson plan development, and other educational theory. This training is essential, but it is also incomplete. Many new teachers enter the classroom underprepared to create high-trust relationships with their students. They are not given sufficient training about the importance of developing relationships with their students or the importance of continually developing one's own character.

The development of powerful lesson plans is desirable, but the quality of the teacher-student relationship is the foundation of a deeper learning experience. Think of it this way: before you can plant a seed and expect it to grow, you must take the time to prepare the soil and create the best opportunity for the seed to flourish. Establishing relationships and creating a culture where everyone feels valued is the key to student and teacher engagement. When we are valued, we will contribute, whether it's in a classroom, a family, or a relationship.

> **The development of powerful lesson plans is desirable, but the quality of the teacher-student relationship is the foundation of a deeper learning experience.**

No Shortcuts

> Don't worry that children never listen to you. Worry that they are always watching you.
>
> —Robert Fulghum

A climate for learning is rooted in principle-centered modeling. Whether consciously or not, all great teachers consistently model principles; a teacher who "lives" honesty, integrity, empathy, love, respect, hard work, and responsibility, basically mirroring our own character development, owns the foundation for making genuine connections with her students.

In today's world, we live in a "microwave society"; the perception is that everyone is looking for the quick fix, a shortcut to success. Many schools operate from a quick-fix, reactive mindset. New programs are introduced all the time. In a school with low math scores, switching textbooks could be a quick-fix approach. However, a year later, if math scores have not improved, the school administration will begin to look for another quick-fix solution. In many cases, solutions to educational challenges have less to do with the curriculum and more to do with the culture of the classroom. Remember, classrooms do not behave; people do.

To become a better teacher, you need to focus on your own personal development (which is a continuous journey). Great teachers don't wish their students were better; great teachers look for ways to become better themselves. Continue to hone your skills as an educator.

> **Great teachers don't wish their students were better; great teachers look for ways to become better themselves.**

Unfortunately, in today's society, too many people seek instant gratification and quick-fix solutions to complex problems. Our society consistently feeds young minds the idea that unethical behavior is not only okay but sometimes to be encouraged. The twelfth grader competing to become valedictorian may be tempted to take short cuts to surpass the competition. Students may learn that lying, cheating, or bullying other students is acceptable behavior. In an effort to maximize their physical gifts, athletes may be tempted to use performance-enhancing drugs. Given this reality, the need for principle-centered role models and trustworthy teachers is greater than ever.

Proactivity Works

> "I've come to a frightening conclusion that I'm the decisive element in the classroom. It's my personal approach that creates the climate. It's my daily mood that makes the weather. As a teacher, I possess a tremendous power to make a child's life miserable or joyous. I can be a tool of torture or an instrument of inspiration. I can humiliate or humor, hurt or heal. In all situations, it is my response that decides whether a crisis will be escalated, or de-escalated and a child is humanized or dehumanized."
>
> —Haim Ginott

Within many low-trust schools, people often practice finger-pointing. In the classroom, the reactive teacher may blame problems on challenging students, uninvolved parents, or the school's weak administration. In a class where a culture of caring has not been established, the reactive teacher may quickly move to extrinsic motivators in an attempt to control the class. When extrinsic motivators don't work, he may move to intimidating strategies such as yelling louder or sending students to the office. Once you begin the pattern, you have essentially lost influence with your students and your colleagues.

The inspirational teacher takes a more proactive approach. This person has a vision for what she wishes to accomplish with her students and takes time to self-reflect and consider ways in which she may be contributing to the current situation. Such teachers are constantly looking at themselves as the solution and not placing blame elsewhere.

To many authoritative, controlling teachers, this approach may seem soft. They believe that students should obey them because they are the "teacher." If students don't obey, these teachers will go back to their old habit of intimidation. They will scare students into following their rules. There may have been a time in the evolution of our society when this approach worked with the masses, but those days are gone. Classroom leadership is about empowerment; it's about gradually releasing your students, not control.

The Whole-Student Approach

> A teacher who is attempting to teach without inspiring the pupil with a desire to learn is hammering on cold iron.
>
> —Horace Mann

The idea of moving from this authoritative approach to a more "whole-student" approach is nothing new. Great educational thought leaders such as Stephen R. Covey, Carol Dweck, Robert Marzano, Michael Fullan, and Richard Dufour have supported this philosophy for years.

However, the reality of high-stakes testing, assessments, and evaluations is putting so much pressure on teachers that they feel the need to "teach to the test." This is a huge issue and a very real challenge. However, research proves that the ability to establish a caring culture, provide leadership opportunities, and give students a voice in classroom decisions will develop the whole student and ultimately improve student achievement.

The tools and strategies that provide the foundation for the whole student approach are the four characteristics of the inspirational teacher: modeling principles, demonstrating respect, genuine listening, and building high-trust relationships.

The Power of Modeling: Second-Grade Inspirational Teacher

Lansford was the youngest member of a family well known to the county social service and law enforcement agencies. His older brothers were notorious in high school for violent behavior, which was met with futile attempts at disciplinary actions and numerous expulsions. Contacts with the parents often ended with threats of violence against the teacher if anything "went wrong" for the boys at school.

Lans's self-portrait, drawn the first hour of second grade, featured a huge head with a double-row grimace of shark teeth. Claw-like hands were shown holding a knife in front of the body. During the first recess of that day, he seized a smaller classmate and threw him to the ground from the top of the monkey bars because he "wanted to be up there." He was quite surprised that the teacher objected.

It was essential both for the safety of the other children and for Lansford's development that some model of acceptable behavior be presented and instituted. The teacher explained that other people had feelings too and that hurting people would not be allowed. After about six weeks of mostly walking the playground with the teacher and more than a few abortive attempts at playground freedom, Lans gradually learned how to play without other people getting hurt.

This accomplishment required consistent modeling on the part of the teacher and the sacrifice of what should have been planning periods with other teachers supervising the playground. It was a good investment. Lans did learn what kind of behavior was acceptable and how to manage disagreements without violence. The improvement carried over to other aspects of Lans's school life, including his academic achievement and his behavior in music and art classes and in the lunchroom. Lansford was not unintelligent and was able to appreciate the increased freedom and comfort his improved behavior earned. He was the only member of his family to successfully complete high school, the only one of the brothers not incarcerated or dead at a young age.

Although bringing about these changes took time and patience, Lans's success was a direct result of his teacher's consistent modeling and her belief in Lansford.

The Authentic versus the Inauthentic Teacher

Live in such a way that you would not be ashamed to sell your parrot to the town gossip.

—Will Rogers

We are modeling all the time; you cannot not model. We are consistently modeling the principles, attitudes, and behaviors we expect from our students. In this section we compare the effects of inauthentic modeling and those of authentic modeling.

The Inauthentic Teacher

Inauthentic teachers treat their profession as a job. They have little or no emotional investment in their students. Their students do not feel they have a voice, nor do they feel valued. Inauthentic teachers use controlling language and begin to adopt a victim mentality, constantly blaming their students or their administrator. Research now shows that the more reactive language we use, the more we begin to become a reactive person.

Inauthentic teachers use fear and intimidation to gain or maintain "control" of their classroom. They have the paradigm that this is "my" classroom, not "our" classroom. They are the ones who hand out discipline referrals like candy. If you want to show your administrator that you are struggling with classroom management, send your students to the office. Inspirational teachers rarely if ever send students to the office.

The Authentic Teacher

> Watch your thoughts; they become words.
> Watch your words; they become actions.
> Watch your actions; they become habits.
> Watch your habits; they become character.
> Watch your character; it becomes your destiny.
>
> —Lao-Tze

Authentic teachers model principles such as integrity, honesty, and responsibility. They are connected to their mission, and their students believe that they are valued, respected, and empowered.

Everyone reading this book can reflect back on someone who had a major positive impact on his or her life. What did these people do? What made them so unforgettable? They walked the talk, they modeled principles, they treated their students respectfully, and they genuinely listened. Over time, authentic teachers build high-trust relationships that unlock student potential.

These teachers recognize that learning is not simply the result of instruction; rather, learning occurs when students are challenged. Students intrinsically want to learn when the content is relevant. Authentic teachers use releasing empowering language and ask open-ended questions. They continually reflect on their own teaching style and continue to improve.

The Need for New Thinking

> Man cannot discover new oceans unless he has the courage to lose sight of the shore.
>
> —Andre Gide

Albert Einstein said, "You can't solve your current problems with the same level of thinking that created them." Effective educators recognize and understand the power of new mindsets and the need to be relevant.

For example, great teachers (leaders) come from the mindset that leadership is about release (gradual release), not control. Challenge yourself to develop a mindset where the climate of the classroom is one of release rather than control, one where students have opportunities to explore, to challenge, to take risks; where students set and track their own goals; where students choose various classroom leadership roles.

Challenge yourself to develop a mindset where the climate of the classroom is one of release rather than control.

Other educational thought leaders, such as John Hattie, Carol Dweck, and Paul Tough, share similar messages. Strive for a classroom where every student can learn through application and experience, where teachers teach through dialogue not monologue, where educators believe that every student has the potential within them. Words like "grit," "curiosity," and "character" become commonplace in the classroom.

This is what authentic teachers do; this is how you become inspirational.

Getting to Know the Real James

By a High School Inspirational Teacher

Ms. Smith was in her fifth year of teaching high school English. She noticed that James, a known thief, was on her class roster. She had heard the rumors of how he would steal, and she was ready for him. This is her story.

"During the third week of school, I caught him taking someone's running shoes. I caught him red-handed, and now I was calling in the campus police. During the interrogation James said nothing and gave no explanation. About a week later, I was called in to meet with my administrator, the campus police, and James.

The police shared James's life challenges. James's mother was a long-time drug addict. He and his younger siblings struggled to find food because their mother spent their money on drugs. James, being the oldest sibling, decided to steal in order for him and his siblings to survive. He would use the money to buy food for his brother and two sisters.

I was astonished. First of all, I was angry at their mother for putting her children through this experience, and then my anger shifted toward myself. I started asking myself, 'How could I be so short-sighted? How did I miss these warning signs? What could I have done differently?'

The charges against James were dropped. James and his siblings moved in with his aunt. Because of my changed paradigm I treated James with more respect and understanding. As a result he felt valued and appreciated and never stole again.

This experience made me a better teacher. I became more open with my thoughts and attitudes toward my students. I recognize some students enter my class with baggage most of us would never imagine."

Three Keys to Modeling

Children are great imitators, so give them something great to imitate.
—Lonnie Moore

Connect to Mission

Your personal mission statement represents your passion and your reason for becoming an educator. Your mission is the foundation for everything you do. It is your moral compass. Your modeling is simply an outward expression of your trueness to your mission. Remember the question: do your behaviors match your mission?

Take Responsibility

Inspirational teachers do not blame others or look for excuses. They take the time to examine, to reflect on themselves. They take responsibility for their choices and the outcomes they produce, both in and out of their classrooms. This is where our power and our freedom to choose our responses begin.

Be Consistent

Inspirational teachers consistently model principles such as integrity, vision, empathy, honesty, service, responsibility, and hard work. This consistency is the result of a deep connection with their values and mission. There will be times when you do not make the best choice; however, you can learn from your experiences and continue to move forward. Once again, failure is fertilizer. Learn from your mistakes.

Chapter 4 Summary

Inspirational teachers recognize the power of principles and authentically model for their students and others. In today's somewhat toxic culture, the need to make choices based on principles is greater than ever. Teachers who take responsibility for their own choices and evaluate their own behaviors demonstrate their commitment to principles, and over time, this will create a ripple effect that helps others to model these same principles. It is imperative to understand and respect that this is not a quick-fix solution. We must be patient, genuinely clarify our mission statement, and live according to our specific design.

By constantly working on our own self-awareness and authentically modeling, we can help our students more consistently make appropriate choices within the classroom.

People Will Follow Your Footsteps Much Quicker Than They Will Your Advice

Whenever people feel a lack of respect or acceptance, it is inevitable that they will withhold their energy and contribution to the class, group or team.

Chapter 4 Reflection Questions

1. Describe the whole-student approach.

2. What is meant by "we live in a microwave society," and how is this mindset reflected in education?

3. Who is the most authentic teacher you've ever had? What made this teacher so inspirational?

5

Demonstrating Respect

Be a reflection of what you'd like to see in others. If you want love, give love. If you want honesty, give honesty. If you want respect, give respect. You get in return what you give.

—Unknown

Respecting is the second level of the Inspirational Teacher pyramid. Once the foundation of principle-centered modeling is established, respecting will be the natural consequence.

To become respected, a teacher must first demonstrate respect toward themselves, then model respect toward others. In other words, you must show respect to receive respect.

When discussing respect among young people today, the conversation seems to focus on the lack of respect demonstrated by today's youth. As teachers, we have undoubtedly witnessed the behavior of a disrespectful student. In this chapter we initially look at respect from a somewhat different perspective: we look at how teachers demonstrate respect toward their students.

Respect Is Not Automatic

The secret of education is respecting the pupil.
—Ralph Waldo Emerson

Respect is not given because of your status or title. Respect is earned over time and is based on your behavior, choices, modeling, and communication.

Some teachers enter the classroom thinking they will automatically receive respect because of their position. This is just not the case. Respect is not given because of your status or title. Respect is earned over time and is based on your behavior, choices, modeling, and communication.

The Dividends of Respect

By a Seventh-Grade Inspirational Teacher

Manny was a new seventh-grade student. He wasn't very athletic. Although he was a brilliant student, his people skills were somewhat limited, and you could feel he wanted to be more "socially accepted."

I was Manny's PE teacher. Manny was shy and appeared awkward while participating in gym class. I was very aware of his challenge but never made a big deal out of it. I always treated him the same as the other students. I was hoping that by not embarrassing him, by not making him feel incompetent, I could help him feel safe and make him want to participate.

Gradually, this approach began to pay dividends. In fact, Manny began to participate all the time. During lunch he would be in the gym dribbling a basketball or serving the volleyball. Soon his skills improved. He began to participate, and his confidence grew.

One day, the following year, as I was returning from the athletic field, Manny's father stopped me and expressed his appreciation for the way I treated and respected his son. He said that the respect that I had consistently displayed toward Manny had had a major impact on his son's self-esteem. He said Manny's newfound confidence enabled him to enjoy school.

Later that year, Manny was elected middle school president.

For some teachers, showing respect to the student is a new way of behaving. In fact, some may feel that showing respect may result in more (not fewer) problems. They may believe that showing students respect may be seen as a sign of weakness, resulting in a different set of classroom management challenges. These teachers, who may be holding onto an old hierarchical mindset, will continue to struggle with the current generation of students.

New Software Required

Although principles of success never change, the specific challenges faced by today's youth continue to become more complex. A new, better, and more customized strategy is needed. Using outdated and ineffective educational methods in hope of producing new-age thinkers is as futile as teaching computer science on outdated equipment. Consider the following comments by Bill Gates in a speech at the 2005 National Education Summit on High Schools:

> Training the workforce of tomorrow with the high schools of today is like trying to teach kids about today's computers on a 50-year-old mainframe. It's the wrong tool for the times. Our high schools were designed 50 years ago to meet the needs of another age. Until we design them to meet the needs of the 21st century, we will keep limiting even ruining, the lives of millions of Americans every year.

Just as technology must be updated to meet the needs of today's student, so must our ability to connect with and respect today's generation.

Just as technology must be updated to meet the needs of today's student, so must our ability to connect with and respect today's generation.

Information Does Not Change Behavior

Many schools have posters displaying character words, words such as "respect," "integrity," and "honesty." Many student agendas have "character words for the week." The hope is that by introducing these principles, schools can help students begin to live them. Unfortunately most schools assess only the students' knowledge: "define honesty" or "what does integrity mean?" However, being able to define a principle is not enough; posters and inserts are nice, but in the absence of modeling or consistent application, posters or lessons will have little impact on students. Information alone does not change behavior.

The Illusion of Respect

The authoritarian teacher's thinking around getting respect from students often involves the use of positional power. This produces often only an illusion of respect. You cannot intimidate someone into respecting you. You may scare people into following your rules, complying with your demands, and even completing your assignments, but you have not gained their respect. This outdated approach to today's youth is most often a fruitless effort. Just as we have moved from the chalkboard to the smart board, from the overhead projector to the LCD projector, a higher level of interaction between teacher and student is required.

Outcomes of Not Showing Respect

Often, teachers start dictating to their students on the first day of school. They tell the students about their class rules and the negative consequences of breaking their rules. They immediately create an adversarial culture. As a result, they spend much of their time in positional power struggles. No wonder almost half of teachers leave the profession within their first five years.

There are many reasons that adults may not show respect to young people. The teacher may lack the attitude, skill, or self-awareness to connect in a respectful way. Perhaps the teacher is simply imitating behaviors seen in the past or those of other teachers in the building. Regardless of the cause, the outcomes of not showing respect to one's students are the same and include:

- ◆ Disruptive student behavior
- ◆ Struggles with classroom management
- ◆ Poor relationships between students and adults
- ◆ Teacher frustration
- ◆ Low levels of class participation
- ◆ Reactive behavior toward students and others
- ◆ High stress
- ◆ Reduced time for learning
- ◆ The illusion of power, when, in fact, the teacher is powerless
- ◆ Increased student drop-out rate

Inside-Out Thinking

Self respect is the cornerstone of all virtue.

—Sir John Herschel

Inspirational teachers have an inside-out way of thinking. Before showing respect to others, teachers must first respect themselves. This comes naturally to inspirational teachers because they've given deep thought to their purpose and motivation for becoming a teacher. They have taken the time to establish their personal and professional foundation.

This solid foundation provides the inspirational teacher with an inside-out filter for analyzing challenges and developing solutions to complex problems.

Outside-In Thinking

Outside-in thinkers look beyond themselves for excuses or reasons for their current struggles. They blame students, parents, or the administration. Inspirational teachers first look at themselves and consider how their behavior may be leading to the lack of respect they are receiving. For most adults, looking at self first is not easy; it requires extreme humility and a strong awareness of our own "blind spots."

The Jimmy Story

By an Eighth-Grade Inspirational Teacher

It was my third year as a middle school math teacher when I first met Jimmy. Jimmy was known as the most misbehaving kid in the seventh grade. Although I taught eighth grade, I knew Jimmy and would soon get to know him much better.

My school had the typical challenges of most public middle schools. During a typical day, several fights would break out. Our school resource (police) officer was one of the busiest guys on campus, and he was no stranger to Jimmy.

My relationship with Jimmy began during the last week of his seventh-grade year. You see, we had only two eighth-grade math teachers, another teacher, who was counting her days until retirement, and me. I don't know if I was saving her from Jimmy or Jimmy from her, but I made a special request to have Jimmy in my class the following year.

After making this request, I saw Jimmy in the hallway and called him over. He said, "What, I didn't do anything!" I said, "Hey, no problem, Jimmy. I just wanted to introduce myself. My name is Mr. Moore, and I've made a special request to have you in my math class next year." He looked at me with a perplexed look as if to say, "But I'm Jimmy?" I then shook his hand and said, "Have a great summer, I'll see you in the fall." As I walked away, I looked back at Jimmy. He was still standing there with that perplexed look on his face. I didn't know it at the time, but this 45-second introduction would serve as the foundation for an amazing turnaround.

A bizarre thing happened in the fall. Jimmy showed up! On the first day of school, he shook my hand at the door and sat in the front row. He had paper, pencils, and a folder . . . labeled "Math, with Mr. Moore."

During that year, Jimmy was the most curious and well-mannered student in his class. He would often hang out after class just to chat. Because of Jimmy's reputation and "power of influence," other students began to change. These students, who once couldn't multiply fractions with unlike denominators, were correctly using the Pythagorean Theorem. Amazing!

Jimmy earned a "B" in my class that year. And it all started with a 45-second introduction.

Unconditional Respect

Showing unconditional respect to your students will give them permission to respect you in return. This may sound easy, but the unconditional and consistent application of this paradigm requires extreme patience and dedication.

"How can I show respect to a disrespectful student?" The greater the challenge, the greater the need for respect. Patience, authentic modeling, and listening are the steps that will make connecting with such students possible. This process will take time, patience, courage, and persistence; change will not happen overnight. This scenario plays out in the movie *Good Will Hunting*. Will's counselor (played by Robin Williams) spends countless hours attempting to break through, often just watching the clock tick. However, by patiently giving respect and listening respectfully, he is finally able to connect and break through.

Examples of ways inspirational teachers can show respect include:

◆ Value your students.
◆ Do not embarrass others.

◆ Do not use condescending language.
◆ Be consistent.
◆ Create a safe and warm atmosphere.
◆ Be a patient listener.
◆ Set clear expectations.
◆ Ask for and value student input language.
◆ Be fair.
◆ Create an environment where risk-taking is encouraged.
◆ Demonstrate appropriate nonverbal communication.

Five Natural Outcomes of Showing Respect

Being considerate of others will take your children further in life than any college degree.

—Marian Wright Edelman

Outcome 1: The teacher will make a difference.

If you were to ask most beginning teachers why they chose the teaching profession, the most common response would be, "I want to make a difference in students' lives." While this is a very sincere and noble comment, many teachers lose sight of their purpose; it can get buried under other "stuff" that they did not realize as they were entering the profession. However, by consistently demonstrating the principle of respect, staying true to your mission, you will make a difference.

Outcome 2: Students' self-worth will increase.

Studies show that improving student confidence, self-esteem, and worth comes from the quality of relationships between the student and the adults (teachers and parents) who play signifi-cant roles in their lives. Such students display an attitude that says, "I am proud of myself."

*Students value themselves to
the degree that they have been valued.*

Outcome 3: The classroom culture will improve.

By modeling self-respect and respect for others, you are building the foundation for a respectful classroom culture. As a result, you will decrease behavioral issues within the classroom. Over time, this will create a ripple effect that will ultimately be felt throughout the school.

Outcome 4: Attendance will improve.

When we consistently and genuinely demonstrate respect, we create an environment where students "want" to be. One of the deepest human needs is to be valued (respected). When we consistently feel valued in a given environment, we want to be there. In a classroom setting, this manifests as an increase in attendance.

Outcome 5: Student achievement will improve.

When students respect the teacher, they are open to new learning. Respect yields trust. In the high-trust classroom, there is less need to control and more freedom to explore more creative methodologies. Higher academic performance will be a natural consequence.

Three Keys to Showing Respect

- ◆ **Connect to your mission.**

  - ◆ Your personal mission statement represents your passion for becoming an educator. This personal blueprint provides the foundation for everything you do. Showing respect to others will be a natural extension of your well-thought-out mission statement.

- ◆ **Respect yourself, then others.**

  - ◆ Self-respect is at the heart of respecting others. Through awareness of your own strengths and weaknesses, you can appreciate the strengths and weaknesses of others. Your behavior and choices say more to your students

than anything you say verbally. If you model principles such as honesty, hard work, integrity, respect, and
responsibility, your students will be more inclined to
demonstrate respect toward you.

Your students will follow your footsteps
much quicker than they will your advice.

◆ **Follow the Golden Rule.**

   ◆ Treat people the way you would like to be treated. Be
   fair and consistent in your behavior toward others. Treat
   all your students with both kindness and consideration.

Chapter 5 Summary

Achieving the respect of your students does not come from your
position or status. It comes as a result of valuing and believing
in them. Before you can genuinely and consistently demonstrate
respect toward others, you must first take the time required to
respect yourself.

You need to continually reflect daily on your mission, your
attitude, and your behaviors. If this process is not given the
sufficient time and effort, your efforts to respect others will be
inconsistent and insincere. To establish your sincerity, you will
need to be patient with yourself; you will need to model the
behaviors and principles you wish to nurture within your
students.

As Emerson so eloquently states, "It is one of the most beautiful compensations of this life that no man can sincerely help
another without helping himself." The same is true for respect.

Chapter 5 Reflection Questions

1. What is meant by the illusion of respect?

2. What is the difference between inside-out thinking and outside-in thinking?

3. What are the five natural outcomes of showing respect?

    1.
    2.
    3.
    4.
    5.

6

Genuine Listening

The greatest compliment that was ever paid to me was when someone asked me what I thought and attended my answer.
—Henry David Thoreau

The ability to effectively listen may be the most important attribute of inspirational teachers. This is the key to gaining your students' trust and respect and to establishing a culture in which they truly feel valued.

The four main areas of communication are reading, writing, speaking, and listening. We have spent many years in school learning how to read and write. However, how much time have we spent learning how to listen? Many of us believe we have mastered this skill; we have "heard" our whole lives. We feel we already know how to listen, but do we? As a result, many of us have developed poor listening habits. In this chapter, you learn the skill and power of genuine listening, which builds upon the previous two chapters.

The Skill of Listening

Listening is improved through ongoing self-reflection, dedication, and humility. Think of ways to enhance this skill; think of how you can continue to become more deliberate and intentional with your own desire to listen. Your students need to know your intent is sincere and that you are attentive when they are speaking. It is through the combination of authentic modeling, respecting, and effective listening that high-trust relationships and high-trust classrooms will be formed and through these high-trust relationships that the doors to student success will be opened.

How We Listen

> One of the greatest gifts you can give to anyone is the gift of attention.
>
> —Jim Rohn

The graph in Figure 6.1 describes how most of us listen with the intent to respond, instead of listening to listen. This is the way most of us listen. Notice that, as someone begins to speak, our attention level increases, then decreases; then, as we prepare our response, our attention increases, not because we are listening but because we are looking for a place to share what we know.

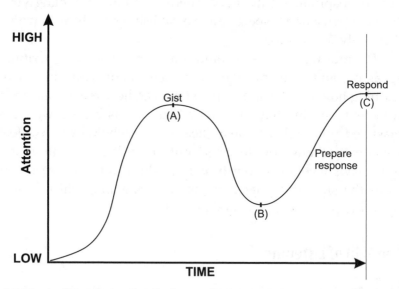

FIGURE 6.1 Listening to Respond

Point A: At this point you (the listener) feel you understand the gist of what the other person is saying, so your attention begins to wane.

Point B: At this point, rather than truly listening, your mind begins to wander. You may begin to think about your "to-do list" or today's faculty meeting, or you may begin to prepare a response to the speaker.

Once your response is "loaded," your attention once again begins to increase (moving from point B to point C). Now, you begin to look for an entry point into the conversation. This entry point could be a pause or simply a breath by the speaker.

Point C: Once the entry point is detected, you "jump in" and let the person know what you know.

This is not effective listening; this is listening to respond. Remember, listening is an ongoing process. We need to practice to improve.

The Frustration of Not Being Understood

How does it feel when you are not understood? How do you feel when someone starts telling you what to do before having truly heard you, trying to solve your problems without thoroughly understanding them?

Why would a teacher not genuinely listen to her students? Consider these reasons:

Efficiency: Teachers may feel the need to be efficient in the classroom, to solve problems quickly and keep moving.

Stress: Teachers feel stress from testing, government mandates, or performance evaluations.

Time: Teachers may feel they have too many students and too little time to listen to all of them.

Distractions: Teachers may have too many things preoccupying their minds.

Regardless of the reason, ineffective listening is the root of many classroom management challenges. These challenges range from

While ineffective listening can fuel a crisis, effective listening can defuse the situation before it occurs.

not recognizing learning gaps to not recognizing a potentially serious bullying situation. The inspirational teacher is tuned in to his students on a higher level and senses things that other teachers may miss. While ineffective listening can fuel a crisis, effective listening can defuse the situation before it occurs. Effective listening allows students to feel safe and empowered.

Think about your own listening skills. Do you listen to understand, or do you listen to respond? Like it or not, many of us are great responders but poor listeners. Why? Many of us underestimate the importance and the power of developing our own listening skills. We typically do not take the time to truly listen before we start offering advice. We assume we understand and jump in to solve the other person's problem (see Figure 6.2).

The Four Listening Styles

There are four listening styles:

   Pretend listening: Pretend listeners attempt to create the appearance of listening, but their mind is actually occupied with a distraction or another thought.
   Selective listening: Selective listeners choose the specific words they want to hear and run with it. They assume they know what the speaker is talking about and jump in.
   Listening to fix: Teachers listen with the intent to solve the problem for their students. The teacher (with the best of intentions) prematurely prescribes solutions to the student's problem. She begins to:

   ◆ **Ask questions:** "Did you ask anyone for help?"
   ◆ **Judge:** "Why wouldn't you do it this way?"
   ◆ **Agree or disagree:** "I understand what you're saying, but I think you're making the wrong choice."
   ◆ **Give advice:** "If it were me, here's what I would do . . . "

Do not misunderstand; listening to fix is an effective skill and a valuable tool most of the time. However, there are times when it does not work.

> *If a student is emotionally charged up, listening to fix will not work.*

Listening to feel: This powerful listening option involves your eyes, ears, and heart. You choose to become an "empathy listener" when the other person is emotionally charged up. The goal is not to provide solutions but to let the person feel she has been heard. You reflect what the speaker is feeling and saying, then repeat the essence of it in your own words. Once the person truly feels heard, then and only then will her emotional level decrease. Now she will be able to ask for your help in providing possible solutions.

A Campus Police Officer's Story

One afternoon, the administrator of my school requested that my partner and I check up on a truant student. The father answered the door and explained how his son had overdosed the night before and was in the hospital.

Obviously this was a very difficult time for the family, and emotions were running high. As we listened to his story at the kitchen table, my partner said, "Yeah, I understand what you're going through."

After that ill-timed comment, the father never spoke another word to us! Not one word.

Listening to feel has two parts:

Part I: *Attitude* (want to)
Part II: *Skill* (how to)

Part I: The Attitude

The foundation of effective listening is attitude. It is the listener's intent and desire to genuinely "want to" listen. Your attitude affects how the other person perceives you. In fact, others can sense your intentions. Your attitude sets the tone for deeper understanding. If someone feels you are insincere or manipulative, this will produce negative results. In order to demonstrate that you truly have the proper attitude you must be patient and respectful, consistently model empathy, and show that you truly care.

Part II: The Skill

The skill of listening with empathy involves the use of your eyes, ears, and heart. You are there just to listen, *not* to solve, agree or disagree, or offer advice—only to listen. Great teachers appreciate and understand the power of being an empathic listener. This may be your biggest asset in creating a principle-centered classroom.

Listening to feel is mirroring or reflecting back what a person "feels" and "says" in your own words. You are not trying to solve the person's issue or fix a problem. You are simply giving the speaker the opportunity to express herself to vent or to blow off steam.

This is not easy! From our experiences in working with educators, business leaders, and others, we have learned that this skill presents a challenge shared by all. Even for teachers with the best of intentions, the natural instinct is to fix or solve. Temporarily suspending this impulse and responding from the heart is what's needed.

When to Listen to Feel

Listening in Times of High Emotion

Figure 6.2 illustrates that "listening to feel" is most important in times of high emotion. During these times, the student (or colleague, parent, or spouse) may be irrational or illogical. At

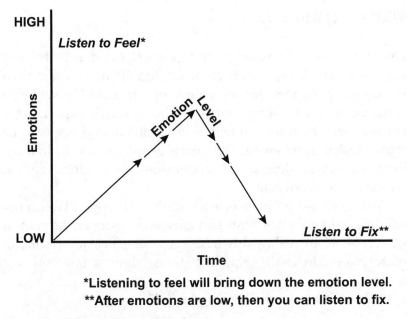

*Listening to feel will bring down the emotion level.
**After emotions are low, then you can listen to fix.

FIGURE 6.2 When to Listen to Feel

this moment of high emotion, the last thing the person wants is for you to offer solutions to his problem. He needs to feel as if he is being understood. It is only through proper empathic responses that the level of emotion will decrease. As Figure 6.2 shows, once emotions have decreased, the person will be open to your input. It is now safe to ask questions.

Consider the following. If an emotionally charged student needs someone to listen to him and you do not listen, what could happen? The student will not feel valued or understood, and the situation could escalate into a confrontation. The results of poor listening could have major ramifications for the student for the rest of the year and even for his entire school life.

How do ineffective or marginal teachers deal with emotionally charged scenarios? Many times they become emotionally charged themselves. Rather than defuse the situation, they permit the situation to become more contentious and possibly confrontational.

What to Say When . . .

One of the biggest challenges in today's classrooms is the way some teachers listen to their students. Too often, we listen from our own experiences, our own frame of reference. If a student's behavior is not in alignment with the teacher's expectations, teachers feel, then the student is the problem and needs to be reprimanded or removed. This shortsightedness results in more behavior issues, detentions, suspensions, and, ultimately, an increased drop-out rate.

Too often we go for efficiency in the classroom. We do not take the time to listen with empathy and discover the root of the problem. In reality, this false sense of efficiency results in more issues. In challenging situations, slow is fast and fast is slow.

What to say when "listening to feel":

◆ "I think what I am hearing you say is . . . "
◆ "So, as you see it . . . "
◆ "What you're saying is . . . "
◆ "You feel (reflect feeling) about (the content) . . . "

Being silent is another great choice, providing the student can tell that you sincerely care and that you truly wish to help.

The majority of times, when students come to you with an issue, what they initially present is not the real issue; typically it's something deeper. However, if we do not give students the needed time and space to discuss (vent), we may never get to the real issue and the student will feel even more frustrated. Be patient, be present, and show you care. One of the most impactful strategies you can use as a teacher is to learn your student's stories.

Be patient, be present, and show you care. One of the most impactful strategies you can use as a teacher is to learn your student's stories.

Scenario 1

Student:	"You're always picking on me. Just leave me alone!"
Teacher:	
Ineffective response:	"Well, maybe if you handed your homework in on time, we wouldn't be having this discussion!"
Effective response:	"So what I am hearing you say is that you feel frustrated that I continually direct negative comments toward you."

(NOTE: the teacher's response should not be formed as a question. The response should be a reflection of the student's emotion and content.)

Scenario 2

Student:	"I hate math. I'm never going to use this stuff anyway!"
Teacher:	
Ineffective response:	"I felt the same way when I was your age; you need to keep at it."
Effective response:	"You're saying that this part of the Math curriculum is something you don't feel you will use down the road."

Remember, your goal is not to agree or disagree, only to let the person feel they have been heard. Once the emotions calm down, they will be receptive to your solutions.

Three Keys to Listening

There are three keys to becoming a good listener:

Connect to mission: The foundation of being an effective listener is staying centered on your mission as an educator. This will allow you to be open, vulnerable, and willing to listen with the intent to understand. You gain your security from principles (empathy, courage) and not from the need to be right.

Attitude and skill: Effective listening begins with the proper attitude. You must let your students know that your intentions are genuine. With this foundation, you will be in a position to effectively listen.

The skill level is the ability to effectively mirror back what the other person is saying in your own words. Reflect back meaning and content.

When to listen: When emotions are high, it is imperative that you listen to understand, not with the intent to solve. Your students know you are there for them and you care.

When the discussion is not emotionally fueled or when the person has had the appropriate time to vent to bring the emotions down, then "solution listening" is appropriate. The student will now welcome your input, your thoughts, and your advice.

Chapter 6 Summary

Listening to feel is a skill that can be learned, practiced, and continually improved. Inspirational teachers know when to offer solutions and when empathy is the best choice. When emotions are low and a student is asking for your advice, he wants you to provide solutions. The student is looking to you for help and to solve his issue. However, when a student is upset, when emotions are high, an empathic listening skill is required. The skill of reflecting back both content and meaning with an attitude of genuineness is the hallmark of an inspirational teacher.

Chapter 6 Reflection Questions

1. What are the four listening styles?

   1.
   2.
   3.
   4.

2. Which listening style do you use most often?

3. When you are approached by an angry parent, which listening style should you use?

Building High-Trust Relationships

The quality of teacher-student relationships is the keystone for all other aspects of classroom management.
                                    —Robert Marzano, *Dimensions of Learning*

As we reach the top of the Inspirational Teacher pyramid, we must remember that only through the consistent and genuine application of the first three levels will we have the foundation to create effective relationships.

Modeling Principles + Demonstrating Respect + Genuine
    Listening = High-Trust Relationships

Given this formula, it should be clear that this is a process, a process that leads to high-trust connections with students. You'll never hear a successful teacher downplay the need for making connections with students. In fact, building relationships and making connections is mentioned in nearly every "teacher of the year" acceptance speech. From valedictorians' speeches thanking students' favorite teachers to the last day of elementary school, when hugs and tears are abundant, inspirational teachers see the evidence of their positive impact on students.

But how to build relationships is the question. The answer lies in the inspirational teacher process.

Kids don't care how much you know until they know how much you care.

The Real Raymond

By a Sixth-Grade Inspirational Teacher

Raymond was always sitting in front of the principal's office. He was a fifth-grade student. I taught sixth grade, and when I would see him in front of Mr. White's office, I would always say hello. I never asked him why he was there or judged him. I simply said "Hello, Raymond."

I was a second-year teacher; the previous year, my mentor (who was outstanding), Dave Lepp, continually shared the importance of not prejudging your students. Therefore I was very cognizant of this fact with Raymond.

Well, guess who was in my class the following year? Yep, it was Raymond. My initial contact with him from the previous year, those simple "hellos," set the tone that he would be valued and respected. He would be treated fairly and not prejudged. I would not allow his past problems and reputation to influence my behavior toward him. I gave Raymond a clean slate, and he recognized and appreciated this fresh start.

Because we established our relationship on the basis of fairness, because no prior behavioral history was used as evidence in this year's class, I never had to reprimand him, no detentions, nothing.

Ten years later I received an e-mail from Raymond. He stated how he had been trying to get in contact with me for the past 10 years. He went on to say how that was the best year of his school career. As I think back, I think it was mine, too.

The Balance of Inspirational Teaching

Although schools and teachers feel the pressure to raise test scores, it is only through a balance of effective relationship building and the skilled delivery of curriculum that lifelong learners will be developed.

Even outside education, today's great thinkers see the power of relationship building. In Stephen R. Covey's *The 8th Habit*, he describes the evolution of leadership styles. He describes *the knowledge age leader* as one who treats others as "whole" people. This leader or inspirational teacher's expected outcomes range from cheerful cooperation to creative excitement. Conversely, authoritarian leaders treat people as things, and, as a result, they face rebellion to, at best, willing compliance. Today's thinking around leadership suggests that treating the student as a "whole person" and not a "thing" is the more effective approach.

To treat the "whole" student requires a significant effort to build relationships. Putting curriculum before relationships is equivalent to the farmer planting valuable seed in unfertile soil. Placing relationships before curriculum is equivalent to the farmer who prepares the soil before planting. After planting, the farmer waters and nurtures the soil. Given these variables and the cooperation of Mother Nature, the farmer will reap a bountiful harvest.

The same is true in the classroom. Great teachers prepare the soil by building trust. Modeling, respecting, listening, and relationship building are the equivalent of sunlight, rain, seed, and hard work.

Impact Trivia (Part 1)

1. Name the five wealthiest people in the world.
   1. _____ 2. _____
   3. _____ 4. _____
   5. _____

2. Name the last five Heisman Trophy winners.
   1. _____ 2. _____
   3. _____ 4. _____
   5. _____

3. Name five people who have won the Nobel or Pulitzer Prize.
   1. _____ 2. _____
   3. _____ 4. _____
   5. _____

4. Name the last five Academy Award winners for best actress.
   1. _____ 2. _____
   3. _____ 4. _____
   5. _____

5. Name the last five World Series winners.
   1. _____ 2. _____
   3. _____ 4. _____
   5. _____

How Did You Do?

The point is: none of us remembers the headliners of yesterday. These are no second-rate achievers. They are the best in their fields. But the applause dies, awards tarnish, achievements are forgotten, accolades and certificates are buried with their owners.

Potential Results of an Imbalance

The success of putting relationships first is evident in schools everywhere. All across the world, great teachers are reaping their bountiful harvests. Their harvest includes fewer behavioral problems, improved attendance, and an increase in student achievement.

Unfortunately, many teachers do not have an effective balance between relationship building and curriculum delivery. They feel it is solely their job to deliver the curriculum and the student's job to learn it. It is this imbalance that creates many of the teacher's challenges.

The results of this imbalance can result in:

◆ Behavioral challenges
◆ Unmotivated students
◆ Low student achievement
◆ Dysfunctional relationships
◆ Defensive posturing
◆ Hidden agendas
◆ Poor collaboration
◆ Guarded communication
◆ Professional dissatisfaction

All children are born geniuses; 9,999 out of every 10,000 are swiftly, inadvertently degeniusized by grownups.

—Buckminster Fuller

Impact Trivia (Part 2)

1. Name five of your most influential teachers (either positively or negatively influential).

   1. _____ 2. _____

   3. _____ 4. _____

   5. _____

2. Name five friends who have helped you through a difficult time.

   1. _____ 2. _____

   3. _____ 4. _____

   5. _____

3. Name five of the most influential (noneducators) people in your life.

   1. _____ 2. _____

   3. _____ 4. _____

   5. _____

4. Name five people who have made you feel appreciated.

   1. _____ 2. _____

   3. _____ 4. _____

   5. _____

5. Name five heroes, stories, or movies that inspired you.

   1. _____ 2. _____

   3. _____ 4. _____

   5. _____

Difference between Part 1 and Part 2

Your long-term impact as a parent, teacher, coach, or mentor is far greater than that of movie stars or sports heroes. Even though you may not always feel the power of your influence, someone will remember your influence (positive or negative) for a lifetime.

Relationships First

Teachers who live with this imbalance between relationships and curriculum inevitably become stressed out, burnt out (either short term or long term), and begin to question why they chose to be educators. Every day becomes a struggle. You can see it and feel it in their body language, facial expressions, and tone of voice. This begins a downward spiral for all parties, from students to other adults in the building.

In the absence of effective relationships, teachers are forced to rely on other forms of "managing" their classrooms. Many use extrinsic techniques such as detentions, suspensions, or fear. Rather than inspire (intrinsic), they intimidate (extrinsic). Unfortunately, too many teachers use this as their primary and immediate means of classroom management. By contrast, inspirational teachers rarely (if ever) need to send students to the office or hand out detentions.

Using ineffective management techniques, forcing students into following the rules (that they never helped create), is a desperate measure employed by teachers who are not completely equipped with the skills necessary to work with young people in the twenty-first century. If you want to let your principal know you have no or little control in your classroom, send people to her office.

A Tree's Spirit

The following story demonstrates what can happen if we continually use extrinsic techniques and go for efficiency rather than effectiveness in our classrooms. The story is called *A Tree's Spirit*.

In the Solomon Islands, in the South Pacific some villagers practice a unique form of logging. If a tree is too large to be felled with an ax, the natives cut it down by yelling at it. (Can't lay my hands on the article, but I swear I read it.) Woodsmen with special powers creep up on a tree just at dawn and suddenly scream at it at the top of their lungs. They continue this for 30 days. The tree dies and falls over. The theory is that the hollering kills the spirit of the tree. According to the villagers, it always works.

Ah, those poor, naive innocents. Such quaintly charming habits of the jungle—screaming at trees, indeed. How primitive! Too bad they don't have the advantages of modern technology and the scientific mind. Me? I yell at my wife. And yell at the telephone and the lawn mower. And yell at the TV and the newspaper and my children. I've been known to shake my fist and yell at the sky at times.

The man next door yells at his car a lot. And this summer I heard him yell at a stepladder for most of an afternoon. We modern, urban, educated folks yell at traffic and umpires and bills and banks and machines—especially machines. Machines and relatives get most of the yelling. Don't know what good it does. Machines and things just sit there. Even kicking doesn't always help. As for people, well, the Solomon Islanders may have a point. Yelling at living things does tend to kill the spirit in them. Sticks and stones may break our bones, but words will break our hearts. . . .

The Tolson Theory Middle School English Teacher

Occasionally someone comes along and pushes the standard of the student-centered classroom to a higher level. Mr. T is that guy.

As a middle school English teacher, he has an amazing ability to connect with his students. He creatively assigns flattering nicknames to each of his students, nicknames like Jones-y, E-dog, Rock, and Skittles. Although they may sound strange, each name somehow creates a closer connection between Mr. T and each student. Even his shy student (Sparky) participated in Mr. T's class.

His energy parallels that of a typical eighth grader. His colleagues jokingly accuse him of consuming a banned substance, but he says his high energy is what allows him to mirror and build relationships with his students.

His approach is simple—relationships first. Although some frown upon this approach, they cannot argue with his results. His students consistently receive high scores on standardized tests. Not only are his test scores high; students have fun and grow emotionally in his classroom. Even the most challenging students tend to excel in Mr. T's class.

The recipe for creating a Mr. T is complex, but the key ingredients are his personal confidence and self-awareness. This guy gets it, and education is fortunate to have him. He is an inspirational teacher.

The Relationship Scoreboard

Imagine going to a sporting event where the scoreboard is malfunctioning. "How much time is left in the game?" "What's the score?" "Do we have any timeouts left?" These are important questions. The players need to know this information because the scoreboard will influence their next play.

There is also a scoreboard for relationships. This scoreboard is a metaphor for the current level of happiness, satisfaction, and trust we share with others. Using this metaphor, teachers can reflect on the interactions of their specific relationships and rate the relationships, give them a score. If the score is low or needs to be improved, you have the ability to make the effort to improve upon each interaction. Every interaction impacts the scoreboard. The interaction can be verbal or nonverbal. Tone of voice, facial expressions, and body language are all ways of impacting the scoreboard. The desired goal is that both people consistently interact in ways that result in a healthy relationship.

Inspirational teachers are like artists; they use different brush strokes for each individual student.

Inspirational teachers are like artists; they use different brush strokes for each individual student.

You will always encounter challenging students, challenging situations. These opportunities provide you with the chance to demonstrate effective relationship building, effective behavior. When you are confronted with an emotional individual, one who demonstrates inconsistent behaviors, this is your opportunity to guide the person, to model behaviors that are effective in interpersonal relationships. The more inconsistent the person, the more consistently you treat him. Consistent modeling, respecting, and listening by the teacher will lead to stronger bonds, and through this relationship the teacher can push the student to levels beyond his perceived capacity, thus unleashing his potential.

A Letter to Mrs. Johnson

Dear Mrs. Johnson,

It has been a long time, so you may not remember me. However, I doubt that you could ever forget me, as I made your life miserable for one solid year. I am writing for two reasons. One, is to thank you for the profound influence that you had on my life. I am, believe it or not, a child psychologist, happily married with two beautiful children. And though I doubt that you realize it, you are the one person to whom I attribute my success. The second reason I'm writing is to apologize for my rotten behavior, stubbornness, and cruelty during the year that I spent in your classroom—a year that would turn my life around. You see,

Mrs. Johnson, I was abused at home. Suffice it to say that my home life profoundly affected my personality, my behavior, and my self-concept. I had no control at home, so I tried to take control at school. The anger inside surfaced in my lazy appearance and that same anger was directed at the most readily accessible adult—you. It always amazed me that no matter what I did or did not do; you never gave up on me. All of my other teachers were such easy targets, I controlled them. I forced them to lose their tempers, to fear my presence, and ultimately to give up on me. But you were different. The louder I got, the softer you became. Though you held me accountable for my actions, you managed to do that in such a dignified way.

The 401(K) Effect of Relationships

If you are planning for a year, sow rice; if you are planning for a decade, plant trees; if you are planning for a lifetime, educate people.

—Chinese Proverb

Many times, as teachers, we do not initially see the benefit in making positive contributions to the scoreboard. Day after day we contribute to the relationship in ways that should produce growth, maturity, and achievement. Unfortunately, our expected outcomes do not always come as quickly as we would like. We call this the 401(K) effect of relationships.

When working with students, you must recognize that your investments may go unrecognized for months or even years. The day your 401(K) account matures will be the day one of your students makes special mention of you during a graduation speech. These are the days you cash in your 401(K) accounts.

In a world where many 401(K) accounts have a zero balance, we must continue to make deposits. As teachers, we

For most of your students, you will never see the results of the seeds that YOU planted. But you will sleep soundly knowing the seeds were planted.

cannot give up. As inspirational teachers, you will have thousands of 401(K) accounts spread across the world. For most of your students, you will never see the results of the seeds that YOU planted. But you will sleep soundly knowing the seeds were planted.

In your life, who has made large investments in your 401(K) account? Your parents, a teacher, or a mentor? Have you ever told them? If not, wouldn't that be a great conversation?

My stubbornness was no match for your infinite patience. My put-downs were defused with your put-ups. As hard as I tried to fail your class, you always found a way to make me succeed. I guess, in your quiet way, you understood that I definitely could not benefit from yet another aspect of failure in my life. I really tried to break you down. I needed to prove to myself that all adults could not be trusted. So, until the very end of school, I never gave up on trying to take you down. Likewise, you never gave up trying to build me up. But because I probably left your classroom with my behavior looking much as it did on the first day I entered it, you probably thought you had not managed to reach me. But, oh, how wrong you were. Believe it or not, I respected you the moment you did not fight back.

I am not attempting to justify my actions. Rather I simply want for you to know what a profound influence you had on my life. What a different place this world would be if all teachers treated all children the way you treated me. And what a wonderful place this world has become for me thanks to one person—YOU.

—With inexpressible gratitude, Jason Winslow

Note: For the sake of anonymity, the names of both the teacher and the student have been changed.

Special appreciation to Annette L. Breaux, author of *101 Answers for New Teachers and Their Mentors*, 3rd ed., for allowing us to reprint this letter.

The Effect of Simple Courtesies, Part 1

While facilitating a workshop for faculty and staff, Tony Contos, a high school administrator, discussed the power of compliments and simple courtesies. He asked everyone to spend the next week focusing on "simple courtesies." He asked classroom teachers to greet students at the door when they entered, to stand at the door during dismissal of the class, and to reflect positively on student participation during the day. He asked the clerical and other support staff to take small steps to greet people positively in their areas of responsibility. As you might guess, the next week, only a few participants were willing to talk about their results. In summary, here is what they shared.

Teachers reported a growing calm at the start of their classes as the week progressed. They noted the change in themselves first (a calmer, happier start) but also noticed a change in the students as a whole. A higher percentage of students were in their seats and prepared for the teacher's instruction during the first minutes of the class. They sensed that the simple greetings at the door and parting comments at the end of the class had created a new beginning in their classroom environment. In short, they were encouraged to continue.

The clerical people admitted that my request did not appear to take into consideration the demands placed on them during a typical workday. Those who told their stories said that their greetings to people entering the office were typically appreciated and that even in the cases when a visiting individual was especially sour (and maintained that attitude through the visit), they (the clerical worker) felt better and not bitter after the negative person left.

The last person to share her experience was a security monitor. She was shy, but she shared the story recounted in the next section.

The Effect of Simple Courtesies, Part 2

The security worker's supervisor had given her an assignment to open a specific door (there are more than a dozen entrances to the school) to the school at the time of day when all students and staff enter the school. This entrance typically sees a good mix of students and staff because of its particular location. Although this individual is kind by nature, she decided to follow my request during the seminar, to assert herself with the objective of applying common courtesies.

Day 1: She greeted people and received a few responses, but while greeting a group of young male students, one young man responded with a derogatory remark. She ignored the comment and continued to welcome the people as they entered.

Days 2 and 3: The greetings continued, but there appeared to be an increase in the number of people responding. The same group of male students entered, and she greeted them as though nothing had taken place the previous day. The one young man did not respond. His response was neutral at best.

Day 4: The greetings were at a high among the monitor, students, and staff. As the male students approached, she greeted them. On this day the one young man looked at her briefly and exchanged a friendly greeting.

Day 5: The monitor was assigned to a different entrance to the school that day because there was a shortage of school supervisory staff. She continued her behavior as she had at the other location. During the school day, she was spotted by individuals who were now used to seeing her at the other entrance (the one used the first four days).

They were happy to see her. They said they had missed her at the beginning of the school day. They were concerned that she was possibly ill and had stayed home that day. End result: she felt good about her decision to apply what we had discussed in the workshop.

Patience and Learning to Read

By an Inspirational First-Grade Teacher

"Tick tock, tick tock" was all I heard as I was making my final preparations for the first day of school. As my first graders entered my room, everyone was smiling and carrying new backpacks, all except one student. That student was Erin.

As other students unpacked, I noticed that Erin was sad. I went over to her, and we talked for a few minutes before she revealed that her parents had money only for her sisters' school supplies. After hearing this, I realized she wasn't sad about her school supplies; rather, she was sad about feeling left out. Later that day, I asked Erin to help me with a few small tasks. She was excited to be my helper, and she quickly became my number one helper. Throughout that year it seemed that she was always there when I needed her.

As the first grading period went by, it became obvious that Erin was a struggling reader. She tried her best everyday, but things just weren't coming together. She was not on level to be promoted to the second grade.

Erin was a very social child and was respected in the classroom. The other students knew of her struggles and expressed understanding and a desire to help her. Soon Erin began to raise her hand and volunteer to read in class. By reading aloud, she improved her confidence. One day, after a memorable conversation with her parents, Erin walked in and said, "I want to be a reader, so I can be a teacher and teach kids like me to read and never give up on them, 'cause you never gave up on me."

Erin passed first grade. It was such a proud moment for her, but an even prouder moment for me. Erin and I had a tearful goodbye, and as she left, her closing words to me were "I hope someone takes care of you next year, just like I did, and if they don't I will be in the second grade hall if you need me to help or teach them how to read."

Keys to Improving Relationships

> Every child deserves a champion—an adult who will never give up
> on them, who understands the power of connection and insists that
> they become the best that they can possibly be.
>
> —Rita Pierson

The keys to improving relationships can be summarized this way:

◆ **Connect to your mission statement.**

Your personal mission statement is the foundation of
everything you do. Your goals, choices, and attitude
are rooted in this life-guiding document. There are two
guidelines to an effective mission statement. First and
foremost, it has to inspire you. Second, it reflects the principles you value. This is the most powerful tool in leading
an effective life and ultimately becoming an inspirational
teacher.

◆ **Value your students.**

The common denominator among all inspirational teachers is the way they value their students. There are other
qualities that make teachers unforgettable—fair, fun,
firm, creative, challenging, and many others. But the one
constant is the way they value their students. Being valued is the greatest human need. Once valued, we reach
new heights and exceed our previous expectations.

◆ **Grow and build the relationship scoreboard.**

There are two keys to building and maintaining a healthy
relationship scoreboard:

◆ *Consistency*: we must consistently strive to interact in
ways that positively contribute to the relationship.
This requires work, patience, and humility. It's easy
to be positive when times are good, but the challenge
is making positive contributions when times are difficult. Your strength during difficult times will yield
major contributions to the relationship scoreboard.

◆ *401(K) effect*: although you may not receive instant feedback when making positive contributions to the relationship, you must maintain patience and stay focused on your ultimate goal of building trusting relationships. As a teacher and mentor you are the emotionally secure and balanced participant in the relationship. This is most important when working with young people or people in crisis.

Going for Walks

When I was working late one night in my classroom, one of my students and his younger brother came knocking on my window. It was Brent. Brent was a low-performing student with poor attendance. When he was in school, he would never talk to anyone and held his head low when he walked through the halls. To me, Brent seemed a bit odd and appeared to have no friends. In fact, I was a little uncomfortable with him in my class.

This evening, he entered my classroom and said nothing. He and his brother just sat in the back of the room and looked at magazines. I asked them what they were doing out at night, and he replied they were going for a walk. I didn't ask any more questions that night, feeling that was all the information he was willing to share. They stayed for about 30 minutes, and then they left.

Over the next three months, Brent and his brother would occasionally stop by. One evening, Brent seemed agitated, as if he wanted to share something. I stopped what I was doing, sat down beside him, and asked if he wanted to talk. He said "no."

Finally, Brent came by and was ready to talk. He took his brother to the back of the room and then asked me to step out in the hall. He shared how his mother was an alcoholic and would come home drunk and abusive. Brent did not want to subject his younger brother to his mother's alcoholism, so he would take him for "walks" in order to protect him. They would usually leave their trailer and walk the streets each night, but when they saw the lights on in my classroom, they came in to get warm. I listened to his story as he opened up to me, tears streaming down his face (and mine) as he shared his life.

The next day I shared what Brent had revealed to me with his other teachers. We all recognized how our misperceptions of Brent were not providing him with the support he truly needed. In fact, we had never really listened to Brent or looked for evidence other than he was a poor student. After this, all the teachers made a commitment to see and work with Brent in a new light. We made sure we listened to him and his needs. We also sought help for Brent's mother.

As a result, Brent excelled. He felt valued and cared for. He believed people were finally hearing what he had to say. Brent ended up graduating with a 3.25 grade-point average. Be aware of the students in your class who also "go for walks." The circumstances may not be the same as Brent's, but their walks are real, and you may never know how your ability to listen may provide a ray of hope.

◆   **Have clear expectations.**

Setting clear expectations contributes to successful relationships. Defining roles and specifically how each person will grow and learn throughout the school year gives great peace of mind not only to the student but also to the teacher. When the relationship mystery is replaced with clear expectations, the teacher/mentor and student are free to proceed and interact with mutual trust and respect.

Chapter 7 Summary

The high-trust relationship is the result of accurately modeling principles, showing respect, and genuinely listening. Once again, this is a process. Discipline, patience, and strength in difficult moments are the qualities that will increase your chances of success when working with young people.

Adults who struggle with this process should look critically at their mission statement, analyze their verbal and nonverbal communication, and take an inventory of their skill set. Most of the time, whenever you think that other people are the problem, that is the problem.

Chapter 7 Reflection Questions

1. What does this statement mean: "When trust is high, speed is fast. When trust is low, speed is slow"?

2. Describe the 401K affect.

3. How do you encourage students to display simple courtesies?

Conclusion

For most of us the problem isn't that we aim too high and fail—it's just the opposite—we aim too low and succeed.
—Sir Ken Robinson, *The Element: How Finding Your Passion Changes Everything*

One of the problems that many teachers face is how to break through student apathy. To accomplish this, teachers have two choices. The first is to use extrinsic means to convince the student to perform. These teachers may make threatening statements such as "If you don't get your multiplication tables memorized, you will not pass fourth grade!," "If you don't pass the state test you will have to go to summer school," or "John, if you don't raise your score in this class, you won't graduate."

This authoritarian approach to student motivation often meets the teachers' short-term needs. However, these quick-fix efforts do not produce long-lasting results. In fact, if you nag students long enough, work may become the course of least resistance.

Many educators have developed an arsenal of punitive measures when students do not learn and consistently conveyed the message, learn, or we will punish you.

—Roland Barth

In view of the information in Figure 8.1, inspirational teachers are needed more than ever.

The second choice involves inspirational teaching. This is the highest level of interpersonal effectiveness and produces powerful results when working with students. This conscious effort to intrinsically inspire others to reach levels beyond their

Top Five Reasons Dropouts Identify as Major Factors for Leaving School

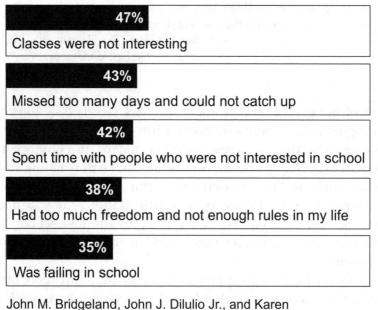

47%	
Classes were not interesting	
43%	
Missed too many days and could not catch up	
42%	
Spent time with people who were not interested in school	
38%	
Had too much freedom and not enough rules in my life	
35%	
Was failing in school	

John M. Bridgeland, John J. Dilulio Jr., and Karen Burke Morrison, *The Silent Epidemic: Perspectives of High School Dropouts* (March 2006).

FIGURE 8.1 Top Five Reasons Dropouts Identify as Major Factors in Their Leaving School

own expectations is desired by many but attained by few. When this approach is consistently followed, teachers naturally create an environment where students feel inspired and open to their leadership.

Motivating students to make the right choices in life is the goal of all parents and teachers. The choices made during the first 20 years of a person's life dictate his quality of life for the next 50 years or longer. As teachers, we have the ability to genuinely impact the future.

The process of becoming an inspirational teacher takes patience and dedication, but the results will be profound for both you and your students.

The Inspirational Teacher Process

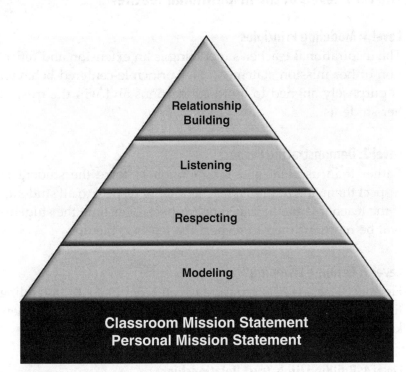

FIGURE 8.2 The Inspirational Teacher Process

The Foundation of the Inspirational Teacher

The Personal Mission Statement

You can see that all inspirational teachers have a solid foundation. They've "detected" and "drawn out" their personal mission statement and identified their values.

The Classroom Mission Statement

The classroom mission statement is created by everyone (teacher and students). This is a statement of common vision and common purpose. It conveys to everyone what you are about as a class. The classroom mission statement should also include expected results, accountability, and consequences.

The Four Levels of the Inspirational Teacher

Level 1: Modeling Principles

The inspirational teacher's modeling is an extension and reflection of her mission statement. Her principle-centered behavior is purposely aligned to build connections and win the trust of her students.

Level 2: Demonstrating Respect

Rather than use fear and intimidation to force the student to respect them, inspirational teachers show respect to all students. If the teacher is the first to show respect, over time the students will be more inclined to respect the teacher/mentor.

Level 3: Genuine Listening

For most teachers, the typical day can seem like a blur. Finding time to truly listen can be tough. However, inspirational teachers know *when to and how to* apply their refined listening skills.

Level 4: Building High-Trust Relationships

Strong relationships do not occur by chance. They are the result of principle-centered modeling, showing respect, and recognizing moments to empathically listen. As a result of trusting relation-ships, inspirational teachers have fewer behavioral challenges, better student attendance, and greater student achievement.

In closing, we'd like to ask you to think of this book as an instructional manual for a brand-new, state-of-the-art power tool. Even though you have read the manual and studied the consis-tent long-term application of the tool, you will not become truly proficient overnight; it will take time and patience. There may be times when you will feel the pull of old habits and go for the quick solution. At times, you may allow emotion to dictate your response. During these times, reconnect with your mission, learn from the situation, and grow. Model the behaviors you wish to see, be consistent, be respectful, genuinely listen, and build, create, and establish your relationships.

> We are now faced with the fact that tomorrow is today. We are con-fronted with the fierce urgency of now. In this unfolding conun-drum of life and history there is such a thing as being too late. Procrastination is still the thief of time. . . . We must move past indecision to action. . . . Now let us begin. Now let us rededicate ourselves to the long and bitter—but beautiful—struggle for a new world. . . . The choice is ours, and though we might prefer it oth-erwise, we must choose in this crucial moment of human history.
> —Dr. Martin Luther King Jr.

You have been given the opportunity to make a difference, to ignite the passion of another, and to change a life. If you've had an inspirational teacher in your life, it is now time to pay it forward. As Dr. King so eloquently shared with us, the choice is ours. Keep the flame burning, and keep it burning bright; you have many candles to ignite.